F. G. Kenyon

Classical Texts from Papyri in the British Museum

Including the newly discovered Poems of Herodas

F. G. Kenyon

Classical Texts from Papyri in the British Museum
Including the newly discovered Poems of Herodas

ISBN/EAN: 9783337179779

Printed in Europe, USA, Canada, Australia, Japan

Cover: Foto ©ninafisch / pixelio.de

More available books at **www.hansebooks.com**

CLASSICAL TEXTS

FROM

PAPYRI IN THE BRITISH MUSEUM

Oxford
PRINTED AT THE CLARENDON PRESS
BY HORACE HART, PRINTER TO THE UNIVERSITY

FROM

PAPYRI IN THE BRITISH MUSEUM

INCLUDING THE NEWLY DISCOVERED POEMS OF

HERODAS

EDITED BY

F. G. KENYON, M.A.

FELLOW OF MAGDALEN COLLEGE, OXFORD
ASSISTANT IN THE DEPARTMENT OF MANUSCRIPTS, BRITISH MUSEUM

WITH AUTOTYPE FACSIMILES OF MSS

PRINTED BY ORDER OF THE TRUSTEES
SOLD AT THE BRITISH MUSEUM
AND BY LONGMANS AND CO., 39 PATERNOSTER ROW
B. QUARITCH, 15 PICCADILLY; ASHER AND CO., 13 BEDFORD STREET, COVENT GARDEN
KEGAN PAUL, TRENCH, TRÜBNER AND CO., 57 LUDGATE HILL
AND THE OXFORD UNIVERSITY PRESS, AMEN CORNER
LONDON
1891

PREFACE

In this volume are contained the texts, or collations of the texts, of all the papyrus MSS. of literary works in the possession of the British Museum, with the exception of those which have already been given to the world. The texts hitherto published are the following: (1) Fragments of a Psalter (Papyrus XXXVII), edited by Prof. C. Tischendorf in *Monumenta Sacra Inedita*, nova collectio, vol. I (1855): (2) the Funeral Oration of Hyperides (Pap. XCVIII), edited by the Rev. Churchill Babington (1858): (3) the Oration of Hyperides against Demosthenes (Pap. CVIII), edited by the Rev. Churchill Babington (1850): (4) the Orations of Hyperides for Lycophron and Euxenippus (Papp. CVIII and CXV), edited by the Rev. Churchill Babington (1853): (5) Homer, Iliad XVIII (Pap. CVII), edited by Mr. E. Maunde Thompson and Mr. G. F. Warner in the *Catalogue of Ancient MSS. in the British Museum*, part i (1881), used by La Roche (*Homeri Ilias*, 1873–76) and Mr. W. Leaf (*The Iliad*, 1886–88): (6) Homer, Iliad XXIV (Pap. CXIV), described in the *Catalogue of Ancient MSS.*, collated by Sir G. Cornewall Lewis in the *Philological Museum* (Cambridge, 1832), and used by La Roche and Mr. Leaf: (7) Aristotle on the Constitution of Athens, published by the Museum in the present year.

The volume now issued contains the texts of three MSS. of classical works which have hitherto been unknown, and collations of seven MSS. of works already extant. The former include seven poems, more or less complete, of the iambographer Herodas (Pap. CXXXV), a fragment of a speech which may apparently be attributed to Hyperides (Pap. CXXXIV), and part of a short grammatical treatise bearing the name of Tryphon (Pap. CXXVI verso). The collations are of MSS. of the third epistle of Demosthenes (Pap. CXXXIII), the oration of Isocrates *De Pace* (Pap. CXXXII), and five MSS. of portions of the Iliad (Papp. CXXVI recto, CXXVII–CXXIX, and CXXXVI verso).

The transcripts and collations, together with the introductions and notes, have been prepared by Mr. F. G. Kenyon, Assistant in this Department. The transcripts have been again collated with the originals by Mr. G. F. Warner, Assistant Keeper of MSS., and the sheets have also been read by Mr. Warner and by myself.

The Rev. W. G. Rutherford, LL.D., Head Master of Westminster School, J. E. Sandys, Esq., Litt.D., of St. John's College, Cambridge, the Rev. E. L. Hicks, M.A., and Professor R. C. Jebb, Litt.D., D.C.L., LL.D., of Trinity College, Cambridge, kindly undertook to assist in the revision of the volume, and their help is acknowledged in the introductions to the several sections which were submitted to them.

Autotype facsimiles are given of a portion of each MS. described in this volume, with two unimportant exceptions. These in all cases represent the actual size of the originals.

                            EDWARD SCOTT,

BRITISH MUSEUM,   KEEPER OF MSS.
   7th July, 1891.

CONTENTS

	PAGE
PREFACE	V
I. HERODAS (Pap. CXXXV)	1
II. HYPERIDES (?) IN PHILIPPIDEM (Pap. CXXXIV)	42
III. DEMOSTHENES, EP. III (Pap. CXXXIII)	56
IV. ISOCRATES DE PACE (Pap. CXXXII)	63
V. HOMER, ILIAD I (Pap. CXXIX)	80
VI. HOMER, ILIAD II–IV (Pap. CXXVI *recto*)	81
VII. HOMER, ILIAD III, IV (Pap. CXXXVI *verso*)	93
VIII. HOMER, ILIAD V, VI, XVIII (Pap. CXXVII)	98
IX. HOMER, ILIAD XXIII, XXIV (Pap. CXXVIII)	100
X. TRYPHON (?), ARS GRAMMATICA (Pap. CXXVI *verso*)	109

ΗΡΩΔΟΥ ΜΙΜΙΑΜΒΟΙ.

Papyrus CXXXV.

It is not often that a literary discovery can restore to us, not merely a work or an author hitherto practically unknown, but a species of ancient literature of which no complete specimen has been extant within modern times. The text, however, which is here published, though not itself of first-class literary value, possesses this distinction; and it also serves to reinforce the growing hopes of a considerable extension of the field of known classical literature. Half a century ago scholars might reasonably have despaired of ever adding materially to the number of works of Greek authors already in their hands, and have resigned themselves to knowing the rest only in fragments and isolated quotations. The discoveries of recent years in Egypt have gone far to open up a brighter prospect, and to raise expectations which, it is much to be hoped, will not be disappointed. Hyperides has come back from the dead to join Demosthenes and his brother orators; and it cannot be necessary to do more than allude to the increase of our historical knowledge from the re-appearance of the treatise on the Ἀθηναίων Πολιτεία, whether it be from the hand of Aristotle himself, as the ancient world does not seem to have doubted, or, as some modern scholars believe, from that of a pupil working under the master's direction. The present discovery has no claim to an importance equal to this. It contains the work of an obscure and seldom-quoted author, and though it presents many points of interest, it cannot be said to be of high literary merit. Yet its very obscurity is perhaps a hopeful sign of what may be looked for in the future; for if a work so little mentioned in ancient times, and therefore presumably so little copied, has returned to light, is there not still better reason to hope that time may restore to us some of the greater and more popular writers, whom we have hitherto looked upon as lost, it may be Cratinus or Menander or Diphilus, or (the highest hope alike of scholars and lovers of literature) even Sappho herself?

The work here published, however, from one of the papyrus MSS. which have reached the Museum of recent years, has a special interest as a representative of a class of poetry of which we have known nothing hitherto except the most inconsiderable fragments. The ἰαμβογράφοι of Greece, with the partial exception of Archilochus, are nothing to us but names. We have indeed several fragments of Hipponax, but none of any length or importance; and for the rest, who knows anything substantial of the others whose names occur in the collections of these *disiecta membra poetarum*—Ananius, Aeschrion of Samos, Phoenix of Colophon, Parmenon of Byzantium, Herodas, Charinus, and many more? Yet they once had a reputation of their own, and were read with pleasure some centuries after they had ceased to write. Of one of them, in conjunction with a poet better known in another class of literature, Pliny speaks thus, in complimenting one of his friends upon his verses (Ep. iv. 3): 'ita certe sum affectus ipse cum graeca epigrammata tua, cum iambos proxime legerem. Quantum ibi humanitatis, venustatis! quam dulcia illa, quam antiqua, quam arguta, quam recta! Callimachum me vel Herodem, vel si quid melius, tenere credebam.' We may, therefore, be satisfied that in the re-appearance of a part of the works of this same Herodas we have a good representative of the class of literature to which he belongs; and as Professor Mahaffy (*History of Greek Literature*, I. 195) finds even his fragments interesting, of which there are only nine extant, averaging two lines apiece, some persons at any rate should be gratified at the chance of testing this sample in a somewhat larger bulk.

Of Herodas himself practically nothing is known beyond what can be gathered from his writings. Even the correct spelling of his name is doubtful. Stobaeus, to whom we owe most of his fragments, varies between Herodas and Herodes; Pliny and Zenobius call him Herodes; Athenaeus, Herondas; and the presumption is rather in favour of a Doric termination having been sometimes altered into an Attic than *vice versa*. As to his date, it used to be supposed that he was a contemporary of Hipponax (6th cent. B.C.) on the strength of a supposed reference to him in one of the fragments of the latter (frag. 75 in Bergk's *Poetae Lyrici Graeci*); but this has been shown to be due merely to a corruption of the text. Bergk identified him with the Syracusan Herodas mentioned in Xen. *Hell.* III. 4. 1, but there is no evidence to support this view. Bernhardy (*Grundriss der griech. Litteratur*, vol. II. 382, 383) makes him a contemporary of Callimachus, on the strength of the passage of Pliny quoted above. Schneidewin (*Rheinisches Museum*, Neue Folge, V. 292–4) suspects him to have lived later still, though without giving much ground for his suspicion.

On the whole, then, we are left to decide the question on the evidence afforded by the poems themselves. Here the materials are not large. In I. 30 there is a passage containing an allusion to a king of Egypt, which, if written 'up to date' as a sketch of contemporary life, could hardly have been composed later than 51 B.C., and may go back as far as the 3rd century B.C. (The references in the same passage to the Museum and the θεῶν ἀδελφῶν τέμενος show that it cannot have been written before the last years of the reign of Ptolemy Philadelphus [285-247 B.C.] at earliest.) On the other hand, in III. 24-26 there is a passage which appears at first sight to require a considerably later date. A father, in attempting to educate his very refractory son, is said γραμματίζειν Μάρωνα αὐτῷ, and this one would certainly be naturally disposed to regard as a reference to Virgil. The context seems to imply that the name was a familiar one, and one which would naturally occur in a boy's education,— conditions which do not seem to be fulfilled by the Maron mentioned in Homer (*Od.* IX. 197) or Euripides (*Cyclops*, 141, 412, &c.). On the other hand, it is quite possible that there is some allusion which would have been plain at the time, but to which we have lost the key. To give point to the passage it is necessary that the boy should be understood to transmute a well-known name into one which was obscure, or, possibly, unpleasantly notorious ; and these conditions may be satisfied in many ways not now intelligible to us, especially since (as Mr. E. L. Hicks has been kind enough to point out) the name Maron was not uncommon as a proper name in the neighbourhood to which Herodas probably belonged. If the reference is to Virgil, the date of the poems cannot be earlier than the end of the 1st century B.C., and even so the passage would be a remarkable addition to the evidence of the immediateness with which Virgil became a classic. In this case the earlier date indicated by the reference to the king of Egypt cannot be rigidly insisted on, as the scene may dramatically be thrown back to a date anterior to that at which the poet was writing ; but it does not seem in accordance with the general character of these poems to suppose that he introduces details which would not at least be within the recent experience of his readers. Moreover, with the exception of the single passage III. 24-26, there is nothing in the poems to suggest the Roman period, while there is much (especially in I. 26-35) to suggest the 2nd or latter portion of the 3rd century B.C. It would be rash to dogmatise on the subject when further investigation may produce more decisive evidence ; but at present it appears probable that the date of the poet will be fixed nearer the reign of Euergetes than that of Augustus.

The locality of Herodas has been at least as doubtful as his date, but the indications furnished by the poems are less conflicting. The dramatic scene of the second poem is Cos (II. 95), and consequently the law of Χαιρώνδης quoted in that poem (II. 48) cannot be referred to the Sicilian and Italian legislator Χαρώνδας. The fourth poem contains a description of a temple of Asclepius, and, as Cos was one of the chief centres of the worship of that deity, this accords well enough with the evidence afforded by the second poem, though the mention of Cos along with Tricca and Epidaurus in the opening invocation (ll. 1, 2) may be held to be against this view. On the other hand, in the fifth poem the word ζήτρειον occurs for a slaves' prison, a name which is stated in the *Etymologicum Magnum* to have been employed in Chios and Achaia (παρὰ Χίοις καὶ Ἀχαιοῖς). In VI. 58 Chios and Erythrae are mentioned, apparently as neighbouring places: in III. 51 there is an allusion to Delos; and in II. 57–59 to Bricindera (in Rhodes), Abdera, and Phaselis. Further, in III. 45 a coin (ἡμαιθον) is named which is stated by Hesychius to have been in use at Cyzicus (though his words do not restrict it to that place); and in VII. 86 the Cyzicene month Taureon is mentioned, together with an apparent reference to the town of Artacé, which adjoined Cyzicus (ll. 87, 92). All these allusions seem to point to the eastern side of the Aegean as the home of Herodas. Nor is the dialect in which the poems are written inconsistent with this view. The prevailing dialect is Ionic, but that is the traditional language of the iambographers, and affords no safe ground for argument. On the other hand the occasional Doricisms, which led Schneidewin (*l.c.*) and others to assign Herodas to one of the Doric cities of Italy or Sicily, are equally well accounted for by supposing him to have been a native of Cos. These Doricisms include the name Herodas or Herondas itself, and forms such as λωβῆται (in frag. 1), ὄρη, ὀρῆς, γλᾶσσα, which occur in the poems (τύ in frag. 2, and κὴν in frag. 4, which are referred to by Schneidewin, disappear from the correct text of those passages); and these are not inconsistent with what is known of the dialect of Cos[1]. It is not, of course, necessary to suppose that the whole life of Herodas was passed in the neighbourhood of Cos or Chios or Cyzicus, and it is highly probable that a writer of any note would sooner or later be attracted to one or other of the great literary centres of the day, such as Alexandria or even Rome; but he might continue to lay the scene of his dramatic idylls in the regions with which he was best acquainted. It is possible that further study of the allusions, proper names, and vocabulary of the poems may lead to some more certain knowledge on this subject; but

---

[1] For this statement the editor is indebted to Mr. W. R. Paton.

meanwhile it must be left with this provisional conclusion, which would make Herodas a follower in the footsteps of Theocritus.

The character of the work of Herodas differs considerably from that of the earlier iambographers. With Archilochus and Hipponax the iambic was essentially 'famosus.' It was the instrument with which the 'genus irritabile' particularly delighted to assail their enemies, and, as both the writers just named were not a little irritable, the iambic, and notably the scazon iambic to which Hipponax was especially addicted, acquired an evil reputation. From these associations the verse of Herodas has entirely freed itself. The metre is the same, the scazon or choliambic, but there is no personal element in the matter of the poetry. On the other hand, Bernhardy's belief that it was mainly of a gnomic description is not borne out by the facts. It consists of short dialogues in verse, representing passages of ordinary life, and intended to be bright, lively, and amusing. There is little or no element of satire about them, but they are not unlike some of the Latin poems which pass under that name. They have not enough real poetry to be called idylls, but the 15th idyll of Theocritus is written in much the same manner, though by a greater master. In prose the dialogues of Lucian afford a parallel to them, though not those in which divinities or historical personages take a part, as the characters of Herodas are the ordinary individuals of every-day life. They do not claim a high rank in the realm of literature, but they are bright and readable, and not without life and vigour. Moreover, they embody valuable details of domestic life and custom, and one of the most interesting describes the visit of some worshippers to a temple of Asclepius, and recounts the marvels of art which they saw within its walls. For the rest, they are not so long but that readers may find out for themselves without difficulty whether or not they are amusing.

As to the original extent of Herodas' work, nothing is known beyond what can be gathered from the present MS. and the few extant fragments. There are only nine known quotations from his writings (besides one which is not in choliambics, but in dimeter iambics), and of these five occur in the poems here preserved; and it is by means of these that the author has been identified, as his name is not given in the MS. The MS. contains seven poems and the titles of two more; while two additional titles (Συνεργαζόμεναι and Μολπεινός) are recorded by Athenaeus and Stobaeus respectively (fragg. 5 and 7). In order to bring the whole extant work of Herodas together, the text of the fragments which do not occur in this MS. is given in an appendix. It may be noticed that a quotation which is assigned by Eustathius to Hipponax is found in one of the poems of Herodas here given (V. 74, 75); but whether Eustathius is wrong or Herodas is using a quotation from the older poet, cannot be determined.

Before giving a short summary of the contents of these poems, with the view of illustrating their general character, it is right to describe the MS. in which they are preserved. It has been divided, for purposes of mounting, since it came into the possession of the Museum; but previous to this division it consisted of a single long roll of papyrus, measuring 14 ft. 6 in. in length and 5 inches in height. For the most part, the papyrus is sound, and the writing clear and in good condition; but in many places, especially towards the end, it has been considerably eaten by worms, and in others the writing has been rubbed, which causes the text of some of the poems to be seriously mutilated. A blank space to the left of the first column of writing indicates that we have the beginning of the roll. and the papyrus is continuous so far as it goes. Its end, however, is unfortunately wanting, and we cannot tell for certain what its original extent may have been. Some small detached fragments of the missing portion are in existence, including the title of one additional poem, besides that of which the first three lines are contained at the end of the continuous portion of the MS. The MS. contains 41 columns of writing, apart from the detached fragments. Each column consists of from 15 to 19 lines, 18 being the most common number. The writing is a small, clear, but not ornamental uncial. There are several corrections by the original scribe, a few in a different hand, and accents and what are apparently marks of quantity are occasionally added in the original hand. Changes of speakers are sometimes, but not always, indicated by a horizontal stroke between the beginnings of the lines. No abbreviations are employed. In the existing paucity of dated materials for early palaeography, it is impossible to assign a date with any certainty to a hand which is unlike any previously known; but the general cast of the hand appears to be comparatively late, and it may be provisionally assigned to the 2nd or 3rd century. It should perhaps be noticed that a portion of one column (col. 41) of this MS. was seen by Prof. Sayce in Egypt, before it came into the possession of the Museum, and the text of it was communicated in a letter to the *Academy* of Oct. 11, 1890. Prof. Sayce states that he was informed that the fragment which was shown to him was found with the mummy of a person who died in the year 13 B.C.; but, even putting palaeographical considerations aside, there is the strongest reason to doubt the accuracy of this statement. If the allusion in III. 24 is really to Virgil, it is impossible that a MS. of a poem containing such an allusion can have been buried by

13 B.C.; but even apart from that it is tolerably certain that Prof. Sayce was misinformed.

The seven tolerably complete poems preserved in the MS. contain from 85 to 129 lines apiece. A short indication of their contents may be useful. The title of the first is 'The Matchmaker or the Go-between,' and the subject of it is the visit of an elderly woman to a young wife, whose husband has been long absent on a voyage to Egypt. It begins with the excitement attendant on the appearance of a guest, and the greeting which Gullis, the visitor, receives on her arrival. Her hostess, whose name is Metriché, reproaches her for not having been near her for months; to which her visitor replies that she lives such a long way off, and, besides, the mud in the streets is nearly up to one's thighs, and she is getting old. After this she at once breaks out into the main object of her call, which is to condole effusively with her friend on the unfeeling conduct of the latter's husband, Mandris, who has been away on his expedition to Egypt for ten months, and has never so much as sent a line to say what he is doing. No doubt Egypt is a most attractive place. Everything that one can want is found there—wealth, philosophy, a great museum, wine, and, as she is careful to add for the better consolation of the deserted wife, women, who might rival in beauty the three goddesses who contended before Paris. At this interesting point the MS. becomes badly mutilated, and we can only gather that Gullis is advising her friend to cheer up and not to 'moor her ship with one anchor alone.' After this recommendation she passes by a natural transition to praise the excellent merits of a gentleman of the name of Gullos or Grullos. It appears that he is a distinguished athlete; he won five events at the Pythian games as a boy, two as a youth at the Isthmus, and since he became a man he has taken two more prizes as a boxer. In spite, however, of all her solicitations and protestations of the passionate admiration which is disturbing the peace of mind of this desirable young man, the younger woman flatly refuses her suggestions, telling her that she would not have listened to any other person so long; and with another mutilated passage, of which the drift is not clear, the poem concludes.

The second piece bears the title of Πορνοβοσκός, or the Pandar; and it consists of a spirited speech by a member of the unsavoury profession indicated, in support of an action for assault which he is bringing against a man of superior position named Thales. It appears that the latter has violently forced his way into the prosecutor's house and abstracted one of its inmates; and the speaker begins by emphasising the point that the jury must not be influenced by the different social status of the two parties. If one man, just because he is a rich merchant and wears a good coat, may assault and plunder another whose clothes are ragged and whose boots are out at heel, then the boasted liberty of the subject is a snare and a delusion. And what is this Thales after all? Not a real citizen, but a mere Phrygian who has changed his name; and it is he that has thus thrown to the winds all respect for constituted law and authority. The law of Chaerondes on the subject of assault is then read, at the request of the prosecutor; and he then proceeds to abuse the defendant's character, in accordance with the best Athenian precedents, though not with equal length or scurrility. He next calls as witness one of the girls living in his house, to give evidence as to the injuries which she suffered by the defendant's violence. He fairly and freely confesses the lowness of his own origin and calling, but offers, if necessary, to submit himself to the torture in proof of his accusations. Finally in a rhetorical peroration he reminds the jury that in his humble person they are trying the cause of all the aliens resident in the city of Cos, and bids them remember the treatment which strangers in early times, such as Heracles and Asclepius, had received at their hands, and to judge righteous judgment, reflecting that, after all, according to the proverb, a Phrygian is one of those articles which 'the more you beat them, the better they be.'

The third poem is entitled 'The Schoolmaster.' A mother appears before the schoolmaster Lampriscus, haling her reluctant son with her, and entreating the pedagogue to flog him within an inch of his life. Her son is the terror of her life. He has nearly ruined her by playing pitch-and-toss. He associates with all the lowest characters of the town. As for learning, he will learn nothing; if his father sets him the name of Maron to spell, he must needs turn it into Simon. Anything that his parents with great difficulty teach him simply runs through him as through a sieve. If they scold him a little more than usual, he either disappears for days from the house, or else he frightens them by climbing on to the roof of the house and making faces at them from this perch like a monkey; in this way the tiles on the whole building get broken, and they are obliged to pay for all repairs. In fact, he has entirely got beyond the control of his parents. In this strait his mother implores the help of the schoolmaster to reduce him to order. Lampriscus rises to the occasion, and his methods are summary. He calls for his instruments of correction, which, being made of cow-hide, are calculated to be drastic in their operation. So, at least, the victim appears to think, and the rest of the scene consists of howls and entreaties and promises to be good, interspersed with hortatory remarks from the schoolmaster, while the mother encourages the latter to persevere in his correction, until finally the wretched youth is considered to have enough, though the intention is expressed of keeping him close prisoner for some time to come.

The title of the fourth poem may be rendered as 'A Visit to Asclepius.' It is not, however, a visit to the god in person, but to his temple, in order to make an offering and do worship there. The visitors are women, and the poem opens with an invocation addressed to Asclepius and to Apollo and Coronis, his parents, to four of his daughters and his sons, Podalirius and Machaon, and other associated deities. The offering is a cock, and the worshippers pray for the favour of the god in return. Business being thus over, the visitors proceed to enjoy themselves by inspecting the various treasures of the temple. The mention of these treasures should be of considerable interest to the students of ancient art, and possibly some of the objects enumerated may eventually be identified. One object, presumably a relief, is mentioned which was the work of the sons of Praxiteles, Timarchus and Cephisodotus. The subject of another which attracted the visitors' admiration is described as a girl looking at an apple which she is longing to get hold of —a representation which is known in reproductions on vases, but of which the original author has not been identified[1]. A third is a vulpanser ($\chi\eta\nu\alpha\lambda\omega\pi\eta\xi$) being strangled by a boy, and this is known to have been the subject of a work by the sculptor Boethus, which is mentioned by Pliny (*N. H.* XXXIV. 19). Among others that are mentioned is a nude boy, so life-like that one of the visitors expects to leave a scar on his flesh if she scratches it. After this they are shown a painting of an ox being led, probably to sacrifice, amid a group of people, looking so formidable as almost to elicit a scream from the spectators, which is easily accounted for when they are told that it is a genuine work of Apelles.

---

[1] Mr. A. S. Murray has contributed a note on this passage, stating that a girl looking up at an apple on a tree, and stretching up her hands towards it, as implied in these lines, may be seen on a vase of the painter Assteas (Miller, *Gal. Mythol.*, pl. 114). She is there a central figure in a scene of the Garden of the Hesperides. Round the tree is coiled a serpent; and if we can suppose that this was also the case with the group described by Herodas the appropriateness of it as a dedication to Asclepius would be complete. Assteas was a painter of Southern Italy, a locality which suits one of the suggested homes of Herodas, and it is possible that the temple of Asclepius in which the group stood was that at Tarentum; though this is not consistent with the other evidence as to the locality of the poet. There is also a vase painted by Sotades, containing a similar group; but as the vase is broken it is uncertain whether there was a serpent coiled round the tree in this case also.

At this point it is announced that the sacrifice has been satisfactorily accomplished, and that no worshipper has ever gratified the god more thoroughly than they have; and a combined invocation of the god follows, after which the visitors go on their way rejoicing. It is unfortunate that there does not seem to be sufficient evidence to identify with any certainty the temple of Asclepius which is here described. Pliny does not state the locality of the work by Boethus mentioned above; and though it is known that the same sculptor executed a statue of Asclepius (*Anth. Pal.* ed. Jacobs, App. II. 777), which may have been for the same temple, it is not known where it was placed. It is possible, however, that further research may lead to an identification.

The fifth poem presents a scene of a very different kind. It is entitled 'A Jealous Woman,' and it opens with a picture of the heroine vehemently assailing a favourite slave for having paid attentions to another lady. He begins by protesting indignantly, but his mistress, exclaiming, 'What a tongue you have got in your head, to be sure,' calls for a stalwart slave and bids him bind the offender. The slave hesitates, and the victim begs for mercy, confessing his fault; but the enraged mistress will listen to no excuses, and tied up he is, and the slave is instructed to carry him off to the place where slaves were punished, and to request the officer there to let him have a thousand strokes on his back and the same on his stomach. The unhappy man protests against this as a somewhat excessive punishment for an unproved offence, upon which she retorts his own words of confession to him, which he explains away as having been only due to a dread of contradicting her. This, however, fails to conciliate her, and the slave is despatched with his unhappy comrade, the instructions as to the punishment being emphatically repeated. But hardly have they gone when the woman changes her mind and hurriedly orders them back. She thinks it will be a still better punishment to have the criminal branded on the face, as a sign to all the world. But here her female friends interfere, and, after much protestation on the one side and persuasion on the other, she consents to let him off this time with a caution; and the unfortunate man is once more restored to such liberty as may be supposed to have been possible to an unprotected male under the government of such a mistress.

Of the two remaining poems very little account can be given, as both are much disfigured by mutilations. The first of these, the sixth of the whole collection, has a title which may be rendered 'The Affectionate Friends, or A Confidential Conversation' (Φιλιάζουσαι ἢ Ἰδιάζουσαι), and contains the conversation of two women, in which, after some mutual complaints of the iniquities of servants, the visitor questions her friend with much importunity concerning some much-admired article of apparel (the exact nature of which is not clear), the work of a certain cobbler or leather-worker, with whom the hostess, Metro, is acquainted. The seventh poem is entitled (according to an almost certain restoration of the mutilated title) 'The Cobbler,' and is a continuation of the subject of the last, describing a visit of the same ladies to the shop of the shoemaker there mentioned. The text is, unfortunately, hopelessly mutilated throughout, and almost the only passage which remains intact is one containing a catalogue of various kinds of ladies' boots, which may be compared with that given by Pollux (VII. 85–94). The titles of two more poems are to be found in the MS., one, 'The Dream,' at the end of the continuous portion of the papyrus, the other, 'Ladies at Breakfast' or 'After a Fast' ('Απονηστιζόμεναι), among the detached fragments.

There are many difficulties connected with the interpretation of the poems which can only be cleared up by prolonged study and inquiry. The language is often unfamiliar, many words occurring which are unknown to the lexicons, with others which have hitherto been known only in Hesychius and similar compilations. Besides these, there are many obvious corruptions which may safely be attributed to the scribes of this or earlier manuscripts, and many places in which it must be uncertain whether we have copyists' errors or intentional colloquialisms. In addition to the use of the Ionic dialect, in the present MS. ι is almost invariably substituted for ει. This may be due to the MS. having been written in Egypt, as this characteristic is not uncommon in papyrus MSS., but it is here more universal than is usually the case, and sometimes where ει has been originally written the ε has been struck out. The present edition makes no claim to present a critical study of the text. To have done so would have necessitated a long delay in publishing it, and it has seemed better to put the scholars of the world in possession of the material at once, whereby many heads may be engaged on the necessary work of revision and interpretation. The text has therefore been printed as it stands in the MS. without emendation. In order, however, not to put needless difficulties in the way of reading the poems as they stand at present, the words have been separated from one another; but this is with a full consciousness of the fact that in the more unintelligible portions of the text they will sometimes be found to have been divided wrongly. The dots which mark lacunas represent, as nearly as may be, the number of letters that appear to be lost. Lacunas have only been filled up when the supplement appeared simple and obvious, or when a fairly certain conjecture would complete the sense of an otherwise perfect passage. The notes have been generally confined to what is necessary to explain the condition and readings of the MS. In the present unsettled state of the text it seems premature to compile an *index verborum*.

Dr. W. G. Rutherford has most kindly read through the proofs of the poems, and many corrections and improvements are due to him. He has also made many suggestions for the reconstruction of the text, a few of which are quoted in the notes; but it would be departing too far from the plan of this edition to incorporate all of them in the text, and it is moreover fairer that his work in this direction should appear independently and accompanied by his own explanations. Mr. E. L. Hicks has also contributed much to the elucidation of the poems,—more than can be acknowledged in each individual instance; and some additional corrections are due to the kindness of Professor R. C. Jebb.

The previously extant fragments of Herodas will be found in Meineke's *Ceterorum Poetarum Choliambi*, appended to Lachmann's *Babrius* (Berlin, 1845), pp. 148–152, and in the third edition of Bergk's *Poetae Lyrici Graeci*, pp. 794-7; and it is from these sources that they have been transferred to the appendix which, as already mentioned, follows the text of the poems.

The autotype represents columns 22 and 23 of the MS., poem IV. ll. 53-89.

I.

Col. 1.   Προκυκλί[s] η μαστροπος

θ . . . . . α αρασσι την θυρην τις ουκ οψι
. . . . . . παρ ημεων εξ αγροικιης ηκι
τ . . . . . θυρην εσωδε· τις συ δειμαινις
ασσον προσελθιν ην ιδου παριμ ασσον
5 τις δ ει συ· Γυλλίς η Φιλαιν[ι]ου μητηρ
αγγειλον ενδον Μητρίχηι παρουσαν με
καλι τις εστιν Γυλλις αμμια Γυλλις
στρεψον τι δουλη· τις σε μοιρ επεισ ελθιν
Γυλλις προς ημεας τι συ θε . . . . . ς ανθρωπους
10 ηδη γαρ εισι πεντε κου δοκε[ω μηνες]
εξ ου σε Γυλλις ουδ οναρ μα τα[ς] Μοιρας
προς την θυρην ελθουσαν ιδε τις ταυτην
μακρην αποικεω τεκνον εν δε ταις λαυραις
ο πηλος αχρις ιγνυων προσεστηκεν
15 εγω δε δραινω μ[υς] οσον το γαρ γηρας

Col. 2. [ημεα]ς καθελκει χη σκιη παρεστηκεν
. . . . . ε και μη του χρονου καταψευδου
. . . . γαρ Γυλλι χητερους αγχιν
σιλ[λ]αι[ν]ε ταυτα τηις νεωτερηις υμῖν

1. θυρην: corrected from θυραν.
2. αγροικιης: corrected from αποικιης. Cf. the reading ἀποίκων for ἀγροίκων in the Berlin fragment of Aristotle's Ἀθηναίων Πολιτεία, ch. 13.
3. τ..: or perhaps π..
εσωδε: the second letter is doubtful.
4. ην: it is uncertain whether a letter is written between this word and the end of προσελθιν.
5. At the end of the line, in smaller characters, are the letters νιδος, perhaps intended for a correction of the termination of Φιλαινιου.
9. προς: corrected from παρα.
11. μα τας μοιρας: cf. l. 66, and IV. 30.
12. ταυτην: corrected from ταυτης.
15, 16. Quoted as from Ἡρώδου Μιμιάμβων

by Stobaeus, Flor. 116, 18, where the mutilated words are given as μνιὸς ὦν. Corrected by Meineke (partly after Gesner and Salmasius) to ἐγὼ δ' ἀδρανέω γυιὸς ὦν (Frag. 4). At the end of the line, in very small characters, the doubtful words seem to be given as μυσοσον, i.e. μῦς ὅσον. Possibly the text, as Mr. Rutherford suggests, had μυῖ' ὅσον, which was corrected in the margin to μῦς ὅσον.
16. χη σκιη παρεστηκεν: Stobaeus καὶ σκιὴ παραστήκει (some MSS. κὴν σκιῇ); Meineke κὴν σκιῇ παραστήκῃ.
17. καταψευδου: doubly corrected, σο being written above the termination, and ε again above that.
19. The ι of νεωτερηις has been added above the line.

ΗΡΩΔΟΥ ΜΙΜΙΑΜΒΟΙ.

20 προσεστιν αλλ ου τουτο μη σε θερμηνη
αλλ ω τεκνον κοσον τιν ηδη χηραινεις
χρονον μονη τρυχουσα την μιαν κοιτην
εξ ου γαρ εις Λιγυπτον εσταλη Μάνδρις
δεκ εισι μηνες κουδε γραμμα σοι πεμπει
25 αλλ εκλελησται και πεπωκεν εκ καινῆς
κῖ δ εστιν οικος της θεου τα γαρ παντα
οσσ εστι κου και γινετ εστ εν Αιγυπτωι
πλουτος παλαιστρη δυναμις ευδ[ιη δ]οξα
θέαι φιλοσοφοι χρυσιον νεηνισκοι
30 θεων αδελφων τεμενος ο βασιλευς χρηστος
μουσηιον οινος αγαθα πανθ οσ αν χρηζη

Col. 3.   γυναικες ο[κ]οσους ου μα την [Λι]δεω κουρην
[αστε]ρας ενεγκειν ουραν[ο]ς κεκαυχηται
[την] δ οψιν οιαι προς Παριν κοθ ωρμησαν
35 . . . . ναι καλλονην λαθοιμ αυτας
. . . . . . κοιην ουν ταλαιν[α] συ ψυχην
. . . . . . θαλπεις τον διφρον κατ οὖν λησεις
. . . . . . και σευ το ωριμον τεφρη καψει
. . . . . . νον αλλη χημερ[α]ς μεταλλαξον
40 . . . . . ουν δυ η τρις χιλαρη καταστηθι
. . . . ς αλλον νηυς μιης επ αγκυρης
[ουκ ασφ]αλης ορμου[σα] κεινος ην ελθηι
. . . . μηδε εις αναστησηι

21. ηδη χηραινεις: a spondee in the 5th foot occurs twenty-six times in the 702 lines (some of which are, however, mutilated in this part of the verse) of which these poems consist. The instances are I. 21, II. 9, 19, 26, 40, 41, 69 (?), 79, III. 65, 69, 76, IV. 6, 9, V. 25, 44, 65, 68, 73, 85, VI. 16, 24, 29, 87, 88, VII. 48, 122.

25. εκλελησται: the σ is added above the line. In the margin is some writing in small characters, apparently κυσης and (above the latter word) αικος (which Mr. Rutherford suggests may be part of γυναικός, in explanation of καινης).

31. αγαθα: the last two letters have been added above in another hand.

32. The left-hand portion of this column is almost entirely obliterated.

33. αστερας: the supplement is due to Mr. Hicks and Mr. Rutherford.

34. Above the obliterated beginning of this line προς appears to have been written, presumably to correct or explain the first word of the line.

37. ουν: the ν is added above the line.

39. χημερας: the first letter is corrected to κ, apparently unnecessarily.

42. ουκ ασφαλης: this restoration is due to Mr. Hicks.

ΗΡΩΔΟΥ ΜΙΜΙΑΜΒΟΙ.

```
         με .... αι ... τοδ ... δε αγριος χειμων
      45 ................ κουδε εις οιδεν
         ........ η με ... αστατος γαρ ανθρωποις
         ........ η . αλλα μη τις εστηκες
COL. 1.  συνε[σ]τ υ[φ] ημων ουδε εις ακουσον δη
         α σοι χρ[ονι]ζουσ ωδ εβην απαγγειλαι
      50 ο Μᾰτᾰκ.νης της Παταικιου Γυλλος
         ο πεντε νικεων αθλα παις μεν εν Πυθοι
         δις δ εν Κορινθωι τους ιουλον ανθευντας
         ανδρας δ επ ισον δις καθειλε πυκτευσας
         πλουτεων τ οκ .. ον ουδε καρφος εκ της γης
      55 κινεων αθικτ ... κυθηριην σφρηγις
         ιδων σε καθόδω της μίσης εκυμηνε
         τας γρα .. χ ιερας .. καρδιην ανοιστρηθεις
         και μευ ουτε νυκτος ουτ εφ ημερην λιπει
         το δωμ[α] [τε]κνον αλλα μευ κατακλαιει
      60 καιτ ἀγκαλιζει και ποθεων αποθνησκει
         αλλ ω τεκνον μοι Μητριχηι μιαν ταυτην
         αμαρτιην δος τηι θεωι καταρτησον
         σαυτην το [γ]ηρας μη λαθηι σε προσβλεψαν
COL. 5.  και οια πρηξεις ηδ ..............
      65 δοθησεται τι μεζον η δοκεις σκεψαι
         πεισθητι μευ φιλεω σε να[ι] μα τας Μοιρας
         Γυλλι τα λευκα των τριχων απαμβλυνει
```

46. ανθρωποις: the original reading was ημεων, but ανθρωποις has been written above in another hand; and some such correction is required by the metre.

47. εστηκες: a dot is placed over the last letter, presumably to cancel it.

48. ημων: apparently corrected to ημιν.

49. χρονιζουσ: the supplement is Mr. Rutherford's.

50. The name Γυλλος is enclosed between dots, and in the margin are the letters γρυλ. The name Γρυλλος occurs also in Frag. 5. The beginning of the line is doubtful. A straight line is drawn over the first α; over the second α there is what seems to be the mark of a short syllable, and the κ is corrected to χ.

54. καρφος: corrected from καρπος. γης: the first letter might be a τ.

55. αθικτ... the second letter might be an ε.

61. Μητριχηι: the second ι is cancelled by a dot placed above it.

63. λαθηι: the first letter is very doubtful.

64. οια: corrected from δια. The end of the line is lost by the destruction of the papyrus.

67, 68. Γυλλι ... νουν: cf. Stobaeus, Flor. 116. 24, who quotes this passage as 'Ηρώδα

τον νουν ματην γαρ Μανδριος καταπλαιεις
και την φιλην Δημητρα ταυτ εγω[γ]ε αλλης
70 γυναικος ουκ αν ηδεως ε[π]ηκου[σ]α
χωλην δ αει δειν χωλον εξεπαιδευσα
και της θυρης τον ουδον εχθρον ηγεισθαι
συ δ αυτις ες με μηδε εν φ[ι]λη τοιον
φερουσα χωρει μυθον ος μετρηιαις
75 πρεπει γυναιξι ταις νεαις απαγγ[ε]λλε
την Πυθεω δε Μητριχην εα θαλπειν
τον διφρον ου γαρ ενγελαι τις εις Μανδριν
αλλ ουχι τουτων φυσει των λογων Γυλλις
δειται Θρεισσα την μελαινιδ εκτ[ρ]ιψον

Col. 6. 80 .. κτ ... ρους . ρεισ . τα .... [α]κρητου
και υδωρ επισταξασα δος πιε[ιν] : δ . ωι
τηι Γυλλι πειθι δειξον ου..........
πεισουσα σ ηλθον αλλα .... ων .. ν
ων οὑνεκεν μοι Γυλλι ων α.......
85 ος σοῦ γενοιτο μᾶ τεκνον π.......
ηδυς γε ναι Δημητρα...........
ηδειον οινον Γυλλις ου πε.......
συ δ ευτυχει μοι τεκνον α.......
ταυτην εμοι δε Μυρταλη τε κ ... ιμη
90 νεαι μενοιεν εστ αν ενπνε[ηι] Γυλλις

Μιμιιίμβων, with the variation γυναι for Γυλλι (Frag. 6).

68. καταπλαιεις : qu. for κατακλαιεις ?

69. και : qu. μα ?

71. χωλον : an α appears to be written over the ο.

75. απαγγελλε : the reading is doubtful.

76. Πυθεω : originally written διυθεω, but corrected apparently in the same hand.

77. τον διφρον : written as correction of μητριχην, which had been repeated by inadvertence.

78. ουχι : corrected from ουδε. There appears to be an α written over the ν of φυσει.

79. In the margin are some small characters, apparently κυη with λευ above them.

80. The whole of the first line, and the latter portions of most of the remaining lines in the column, are nearly obliterated by rubbing, and some of the last letters printed in each line in the text are doubtful.

ΗΡΩΔΟΤ ΜΙΜΙΑΜΒΟΙ.

II.

Πορνοβοσκος

ανδρες δικασται της γενης μ[εν] ουκ εστε
ημεων κριται δηκουθεν ουδ[ε τη]ς δοξη[ς]
ουδ ι Θαλης μεν ουτος αξιην τ . . νυν
εχι ταλαντων πεντ εγω δ εμ[ου]ς αρτους

COL. 7. 5 . . . . περ εξει Βατταρον . . . ημ . . ας
. . . και . ω αυτον γαρ . . . . κλαυσαι
. . . . ιης ο μαστος ηιασ . . . ν χωρη
. . . . . μεν . . . . τι της [πο]λιος κηγω
. . . . κως βουλο[με]θα καλλως ημεας
10 . . . . . ος ελκι προστατην . . . μεννην
. . . . ων τα πυξ [νε]νικηκεν
. . . . νης . . . οφων δε κ . . νυν αγχι
. . . . ης . . . . . εα ταυτα τ . . . ου δυντος
. . . . θε . . . . ων ανδρες . . . χε χλαιναν
15 . . . . νως . . . ιωι προστατ . . εθ ωρισμαι
. . . . εξακης ελ . . . . α . .
. . . . ουσα π . . νκή τηστατιν κακην λι . ον
. . . . νας εκ τυρου τι τωι δημωι
. . . . ωρε ην γαρ ουθ ουτος πυρους
20 . . . . θιν ουτ εγω παλιν κ . ινήν

COL. 8. ει δ ουνεκεν πλι την θαλασσαν η χλαιναν
εχι τριων μνεων Αττικων εγω δ οικεω
εν γηι τριβωνα και ασκερας σαπρας ελκων
βιηι τιν αξι των εμων εμ ου πεισας
25 και ταυτα νυκτος οιχεθ ημιν η αλεωρη
της πολιος ανδρες καφ οτωι σεμνυνεσθε
την αυτονομιην υμεων Θαλης λυσει

II.

2. δοξης: it is uncertain whether the s is written or not.
3. Over the letters νυν is written an η.
5. The left-hand portion of this column is torn away, and the rest is much mutilated.

6. αυτον: or λυτον.
8. πολιος: corrected from πολεως.
10. In the margin opposite this line is written the word νεμειν.
16. ελ . . : or εν . .

ΗΡΩΔΟΥ ΜΙΜΙΑΜΒΟΙ.

```
           ον εχρην αυτον οστις εστι κακ ποιου
           πηλου πεφυρηται δοτ ως εγω ζωιην
        30 των δημοτεων φρισσοντα και τον ηκιστον
           νυν δ οι μεν εοντες της πολιος καλυπτηρες
           και τηι γενηι φυσωντες ουκ ισον τουτωι
           προς τους νομους βλεπουσι κημε τον ξινον
           ου[δει]ς πολιτης ηλοησεν ουδ ηλθεν
        35 προς τας θυρας μευ νυκτος ουδ εχων δαιδας
COL. 9.    την [ο]ικιην υφ[ηψ]εν ουδε των πορνεων
           [βι]ηι λαβων οιχωκεν αλλ ο Φρυξ ουτος
           ο νυν Θαλης εων προσθε δ ανδρες Αρτιμμης
           η παντα ταυτ επρηξε κουκ επηιδεσθη
        40 ουτε νομον ουτε προστατην ουτ αρχοντα
           [κ]αιτοι λαβων μοι γραμματευ της αικιης
           τον νομον ανειπε και συ την οπην βυσον
           της κλεψυδρης βελτιστε μεχρις ου ειπηι
           μη προς τε κυσος φησι χω ταπης ημιν
        45 το του λογου δη τουτο ληϊς κυρσηι
           επην δ ελευθερος τις αικισηι δουλην
           η εκων επισπηι της δικης το τιμημα
           διπλουν τελιτω ταυτ εγραψε Χαιρωνδης
           ανδρες δικασται κουχι Ватταρος χρηζων
        50 Θαλην μετελθειν ην θυρην δε τις κοψηι
COL. 10.   μνην τινετω φησιν ην δε πυξ αλοιησηι
           αλλην παλι μνην ην δε τα οικι εμπρησ[ηι]
           η ορους υπερβηι χιλιας το τιμημα
           [εν]ιμε κην βλαψηι τι διπλοον τινιν
        55 [ωκ]ι πολιν γαρ ω Θαλης συ δ ουκ οισθας
           ου[τ]ε πολιν ουτε πως πολις διοικιται
           ο[ικι]ς δε σημερον μεν εν Βρικινδηροις
           εχθες δ εν Λβδηροισιν αυριον δ ην σοι
```

36. οικιην: corrected from οικιαν.
38. Before προσθε is an α, which has been cancelled by a dot placed above it.
39. η: the reading is not quite certain.
40. προστατην: or possibly προσταγην.

49. κουχι: at first και ουχι, but αι is struck out. Ватταρος: at first written βατταως.
52. παλι μνην: thus, for παλιν μνην.
55. ωκι: the remains of the first letter resemble an ω, but the next is illegible.

ναυλον διδοι τις ες Φασηλιδα πλωση
60 ε[γ]ω δ οκως αν μη μακρηγορεων υμεας
ωνδρες δικασται τηι παροιμιηι τρυχω
πεπονθα προς Θαλητος οσσα κημ πισσηι
μυς πυξ επληγην η θυρη κατηρακται
της οικιης μευ της τελεω τριτην μισθον
65 τα υπερθυρ οπτα δευρο Μυρταλη και συ
δειξον σεωυτην πασι μηδεν αισχυνευ

Col. 11. νομιζε το[υτ]ου[ς] ους οργις δικαζοντας
πατερας αδελφους εμβλεπειν ορητ ανδρες
τα τιλματ αυτης και κατωθεν κανωθεν
70 ως λια ταυτ ετιλλεν ὤναγης ουτος
οθ ιλκεν αυτην καβιαζετ ω γηρας
σοι θυετω επ .. τον μαν εξεφυσησεν
ωσπερ φιλ .... εν Σαμωι κοτ ο βρεγκος
γελαις κιν[αι]δ[ος] ειμι και ουκ απαρνευμαι
75 και Βατταρος μοι τουνομ εστι χω παππος
ην μοι Σισυ[μ]βρας χω πατηρ Σισυμβρίσκος
κηπορνοβοσ[κ]ευν παντες αλλ εκητ αλκης
θαρσεων λε .. [λεγ]οιμ αν ι Θαλης ιηι
εραις συ μεν ισω[ς] Μυρταλης ουδεν δεινον
80 εγω δ επυρεον ταυτα δους εκιν εξις
η νη Δι ι σεν θ[α]λπεται τι των ενδον

Col. 12. εμβυσον εις την χιρα Βα[ττ]αριωι τιμην
καυτο[ς] τα σαυτου θλῆ λαβων οκως χρηζεις
εν δ εστιν ανδρες ταυτα μεν γαρ ειρηται
85 προς [τ]ουτον υμεις δ ως αμαρτυρων ευντων

62. κημ πισσηι: corrected from καπισσηι; = και η εν πισσῃ.
64. μισθον: corrected from μοιραν.
67. οργις: corrected from οριιις.
69. κατωθεν: the ν is perhaps meant to be struck out; and this would improve the metre, spondees in the 5th foot being rare.
73. κοτ: corrected from ποτ.
78. λε..: the letter following λε appears to be ω. Qu. λεων or λεωι.

79. συ is added above the line. Two dots are placed over the δ and ε of ουδεν, as though to cancel them, and some letter seems to have been inserted after the δ of δεινον, but it is not clear what it is.
82. An ι is added at the end of the line, but is cancelled by a dot above it.
84. εν δ εστιν: at first written εν δε τις.
ανδρες: corrected from ανδρας.

γνωμηι δικαιηι την κρισιν διαιτατε
ην δ οιον ες τα δουλα σωματα σπευδηι
κης βασανον αιτηι προσδιδωμι καμαντον
λαβων Θαλη στρεβλου με μουνον η τιμη
90 εν τωι μεσωι εστω ταυτα τρυταιηι Μινως
ουκ αν δικαζων βελτιον δ[ι]ηιτησε
το λοιπον ανδρες μη δοκιτε την ψηφον
τωι πορνοβοσκωι Ватταρωι φερειν αλλα
απασι τοις οικευσι την πολιν ξινοις
95 νυν διξεθ η Κῶς κω Μεροψ κοσον δραινει
χω Θεσσαλος τιν ειχε χηρακλης δοξαν
χωσκληπιος κῶς ηλθεν ενθαδ εκ Τρικκης
COL. 13. κήτικτε Λητοῦν ωδ ετ εὖχαριν Φοιβη
ταυτα σκοπευντες παντα την δικην ορθηι
100 γνωμηι κυβερνατ ως ο Φρυξ τα νυν υμιν
πληγις αμινων εσσετ ει τι μη ψευδος
εκ των παλαιων η παροιμιη βαζι

III.

Διδασκαλος

ουτω τι σοι δοιησαν αι φιλαι Μουσαι
Λαμπρισκε τερπνον της ζοης τ επαυρεσθαι
τουτον κατ ωμου διρον αχρις η ψυχη
αυτου επι χιλεων μουνον η κακη λιφθηι
5 εκ μεν ταλαινης την στεγην πεπορθηκεν
χαλκίνδα παιζων και γαρ ουδ απαρκευσιν
αι αστραγάλαι Λαμπρισκε συμφορης δ ηδη
ορμαι επι μεζον κου μεν η θυρη κιται
του γραμματιστεω και τριηκας η πικρη
COL. 14. 10 τον μισθον αιτι κην τα Ναννακου κλαυσω

88. αιτηι: the ι adscript appears to have been added subsequently.
95. κοσον: the first letter is doubtful.
96. ειχε χηρακλης: corrected from ειχεν Ηρακλης.
102. A ρ has been added, above the line, between the β and α; but the alteration would spoil the sense.

III.

10. κην τα Ναννακου: cf. Zenobius VI. 10, where this is quoted as a proverb, with a slight variation. His words are Νάννακος ἐγένετο

ουκ αν ταχεως ληξιε την γε μην παιστρην
οκου περ οικιζουσιν οι τε προυνικοι
κοι δρηπεται σαφ οιδε κητερωι διξαι
κη μεν ταλαινα δελτος ην εγω καμνω
15 κηρουσ εκαστου μηνος ορφανη κιται
προ της χαμευνης του επι τοιχον ερμινος
κην μηκοτ αυτην οιον Λιδην βλεψας
γραψηι μεν ουδεν καλον εκ δ οληη ξυσηι
αι δορκαλιδες δε ναι παρωτεραι πολλον
20 εν τηισι φυσηις τοις τε δικτυοις κεινται
της ληκυθου ημεων τηι επι παντι χρωμεσθα
επισταται δ ουδ αλφα συλλαβην γνωναι
ην μη τις αυτωι ταυτα πεντακις βωσαι
τριθημεραι Μαρωνα γραμματιζοντος
25 του πατρος αυτωι τον Μαρωνα εποιησεν
COL. 15. ουτος Σιμωνα ο χρηστος ωστ εγωγ ιπα
ανουν εμαυτην ητις ουκ ονους βοσκιν
αυτον διδασκω γραμματων δε παιδιην
δοκευσ αρωγον της αωριης εξιν
30 επεαν δε δη και ρησιν οια παιδισκον
η γω μιν ιπιν η ο πατηρ ανωγωμεν
γερων ανηρ ωσιν τε κωμμασιν καμνων
ενταυθ οκως νιν εκ τετρημενης ηθι
Απολλον αγρευ τουτο φημι χη μαμμη
35 ταλης ερι σοι κηστι γραμματων χηρη
κω προστυχων Φρυξ ην δε δη τι και μιζον
γρυξαι θελωμεν η τριταιος ουκ οιδεν
της οικιης τον ουδον αλλα την μαμμην
γρηνν γυναικα κωρφανην βιου κιρι

Φρυγῶν βασιλεύς... πρὸ τῶν Δευκαλίωνος χρόνων, ὃς προειδὼς τὸν μέλλοντα κατακλυσμὸν συνηγαγὼν πάντας εἰς τὰ ἱερὰ μετὰ δακρύων ἱκέτευεν. Ἡρώδης δὲ ὁ ἰαμβοποιός φησιν, ἵνα τὰ Νιννάκου κλαύσω. The latter word has been altered by Schneidewin to κλαύσῃ, and is so quoted by Meineke (Frag. 9).

18. ξυσηι: corrected from ξυληι.

19. δε ναι: at first written δαι, but εν is written above, apparently for insertion.

21. τηι: corrected from την.

31. ιπιν: at first written ειπιν, but a dot is placed above the ε to cancel it.

33. ηθι: corrected from ιθι.

34. αγρευ: corrected from αυρευ.

35. ταλης: or *divisim*, τα λης.

ΗΡΩΔΟΥ ΜΙΜΙΑΜΒΟΙ.

   40 η του τεγευς υπερθε τα σκελεα τινας
     καθηθ οκως τις καλλιης κατω κυπτων
     τι μευ δοκεις τα σπλαγχνα της κακης πασχιν
Col. 16. επεαν ιδωμι κου τόσος λογος τουδε
     αλλ ο κεραμος πας ωσπερ ιτια θληται
   45 κηπην ο χιμων εγγυς ηι τρι ημαιθα
     κλαιουσ εκαστου του πλατυσματος τινω
     εν γαρ στομ εστι της συνοικιης πασης
     του Μητροτιμης εργα Κοτταλου ταυτα
     καληθιν' ωστε μηδ οδοντα κινησαι
   50 ορη δ οκοιως την ρακιν λελεπρηκε
     πασαν καθ υλην οια Δηλιος κυρτευς
     εν τηι θαλασσηι τωμβλυ της ζοης τριβων
     τας εβδομας τ αμινον ικαδας τ οιδε
     των αστροδιφεων κουδ υπνος νιν αιριται
   55 νοευνθ οτ ημος παιγνιην αγινητε
     αλλ ει τι σοι Λαμπρισκε και βιου πρηξιν
     εσθλην τελοιεν αι δε καγαθων κυρσαις
     μη λασσον αυτωι Μητροιτιμη επευχεο
     εξει γαρ ουδεν μιον Ευθιης κου μοι
   60 κου Κοκκαλος κου Φιλλος ου ταχεως τουτον
Col. 17. αριτ επ ωμου τηι Ακέσεω σεληναιηι
     διξον τε σ αινεω ταργα Κοτταλ α πρησσις
     ου σοι ετ απαρκει ταισι δορκασιν παιζειν
     άστράβδ οκωσπερ οιδε προς δε την παιστρην
   65 εν τοισι προνικοισι χαλκιζεις φοιτεων
     εγω σε θησω κοσμιωτερον κουρης

44. ιτια: Mr. Rutherford suggests ιτρια, Mr. Hicks ιτεα.
45. ημαιθα: corrected from ημεθα.
46. κλαιουσ: at first written κλαιουσα, but the final α is struck out.
50. δ οκοιως: corrected from δε κοιως.
52. τωμβλυ της ζοης: *cf.* Frag. 5, l. 4.
53. εβδομας: after the α the letters δα are inserted above the line, but the change destroys the metre.
59. κου: corrected from που.

61. τηι Ακέσεω σεληναιηι: Mr. Rutherford has pointed out that this is the proverb quoted in Diogen. I. 57, VI. 30, and elsewhere in the Paroemiographi.
62. Κοτταλ: a second λ is added above the line, but its insertion would interfere with the metre; and as a dot is placed above it it was perhaps intended to be cancelled again.
63. παιζειν: corrected from πεμπειν.
65. προνικοισι: a slip for προυνικοισι.

ΗΡΩΔΟΥ ΜΙΜΙΑΜΒΟΙ.

κινευντα μηδε καρφοσι το γ ηδιστον
κου μοι το δριμυ σκυλος η βοος κερκος
ωι τους πεδητας καποτακτους λωβευμαι
70 δοτω τις εις την χειρα πριν χολη βηξαι
μη μη ικετευω Λαμπρισκε προς σε των Μουσεων
και του γενειου της τε κοττιδος ψυχης
μη τωι με δριμει τωι τερωι δε λωβησαι
αλλ ἰς πονηρος Κοτταλε ωστε και πέρνας
75 ουδις σ επαινεσειεν ουδ οκως χωρης
οι μυς ομοιως τον σιδηρον τρωγουσιν
κοσας κοσας Λαμπρισκε λισσομαι μελλις
ες μευ φορησαι μη με τηνδε δ ιρωτα

Col. 18. τᾶτᾶ κοσας μοι δωσετ ἰ τί σοι ζωην
80 φερειν οσας αν η κακη σθενη βυρσα
παυσαι ικαναι Λαμπρισκε και συ δη παυσαι
κακ εργα πρησσων ουκετ ουχι πρηξω
ομνυμι σοι Λαμπρισκε τας φιλας Μουσας
οσσην δε και την γλασσαν ουτος εσχηκας
85 προς σοι βαλεω τον μυν ταχ ην πλεω γρυξηις
ιδου σιωπω μη με λισσομαι κτεινηις
μεθεσθε Κοκκαλ αυτον ουδ εκληξαι
Λαμπρισκε δειρον δ αχρις ηλιος δυσηι
αλλ εστιν υδρης ποικιλωτερος πολλωι

71. ικετευω : dots have been placed above the letters ευ, to cancel them, *metri gratia*.

Λαμπρισκε : at first written προσπρισκε, by a slip of the pen.

72. του γενειου : corrected from των γενειων.
κοττιδος : corrected from κουτιδος.

75. οκως : apparently altered to οκου, in another hand.

78. μη : a slight interval before this word indicates a change of speaker.

79. ζωην : the η is dotted, but with what purpose is not clear.

80. φερειν : the last three letters are added above the line. σθενη βυρσα : an ι was originally written at the end of each of these words, but has been struck out.

82. πρησσων : the second σ is added above the line. πρηξω : corrected from παιξω. A syllable must have dropped out of this line, as the metre is defective ; perhaps τι should be inserted after ουχι. Mr. Rutherford suggests ουκετ ου for ουχι.

83. σοι : corrected from αοι.

84. εσχηκας : corrected from εσχηκε.

87. The metre of this line is deficient in a syllable. There is a change of speaker after αυτον, and the syllable must be supplied in the next words. Mr. Rutherford suggests ουκ αν εκληξαις.

88. The δ is added above the line.

24   ΗΡΩΔΟΤ ΜΙΜΙΑΜΒΟΙ.

   90 και δι λαβιν νιν καπι βυβλιωι δηκου
     το μηθεν αλλας ικοσιν γε και ην μελληι
     αυτης αμινον της κλεοῦς αναγνωναι
     ισσᾶι λαθοις την ιλασσαν ες μελι πλυνας
     ερεω επιμηθεως τωι γεροντι Λαμπρισκε
   95 ελθουσ ες οικον ταυτα και πεδας ηξω
     φερουσ οκως νιν συμποδω δε πηδευντα
Col. 19. αι.....αι βλεπωσιν ας εμισησεν

IV.

    Λσκληπιωι ανατιθεισαι και θυσιαζουσαι
    χαιροις α[ν]αξ Παιηον ος μεδις Τρικκης
    και Κων γλυκηαν κηπιδαυρον ωικηκας
    συν και Κορωνις η σ ετικτε χωπολλων
    χαιροιεν ης τε χιρι δεξιηι ψανις
   5 Υγιϊα τε κ' ων περ οιδε τιμιοι βωμοι
    Πανακη τε κηπιω τε κιησω χαιροι
    χοι Λεωμεδοντος οικιην τε και τιχη
    περσαντες ιητηρες αγριων νουσων
    Ποδαλιριος τε και Μαχαων χαιροντων
  10 χωσοι θεοι σην εστιην κατοικευσιν
    και θεαι πατερ Παιηον ιλεω δευτε
    του αλεκτορος τουδ οντιν οικιης τοιχων
    κηρυκα θυω ταπιδορπα δεξαισθε
    ου γαρ τι πολλην ουδ ετοιμον αντλευμεν
  15 επι ταχ αν βουν η νενημενην χοιρον
    πολλης φοριης κουκ αλεκτορ' ιητρα
Col. 20. νουσων εποιευμεσθα τας απεψησας
    επ ηπιας συ χειρας ω αναξ τινας
    εκ δεξιης τον πινακα Κοκκαλη στησον
  20 της Υγιης μᾶ καλων φιλη Κυννοι

91. μηθεν: corrected from μηδεν.
93. ιλασσαν: qu. γλασσαν?

11. ιλεω: corrected from ιδεω.
12. του: corrected to τω, but apparently wrongly.

IV.

4. χιρι: at first written χειρι, but the ε is cancelled by a dot placed above it.

16. ιητρα: at first written ιητρια, but the second ι is dotted, apparently to cancel it.

ΗΡΩΔΟΥ ΜΙΜΙΑΜΒΟΙ.

αγαλματων τις ηρα την λιθον ταυτην
τεκτων εποει και τις εστιν ο στησας
οι Πρηξιτελεω παιδες ουχ ορηις κινα
εν τηι βασι τα γραμματ Ευθιης δ αυτα
25 εστησεν ο Πρηξωνος ιλεως ιη
και τοισδ ο Παιων και Ευθιης καλων εργων
ορη φιλη την παιδα την ανω κεινην
βλεπουσαν ες το μηλον ουκ ερις αυτην
ην μη λαβηι το μηλον εκ ταχα ψυξι
30 κεινον δε Κυννοι τον γεροντα προς Μοιρεων
την χηναλωπεκα ως το παιδιον πνιγει
προ των ποδων γουν ι τι μη λιθος τουργον
ερις λαλησι μα χρονωι κοτ ωνθρωποι
κης τους λιθους εξουσι την ζοην θιναι

COL. 21. 35 τον Βαταλης γαρ τουτον ουχ ορης Κυννοι
οκως β[ε]β..... ανδριαντα της Μυττεω
ει μη τις αυτην ιδε Βαταλην βλεψας
ες τουτο το ικονεισμα μη... ης δισθω
επευ φιλη μοι και καλον τι σοι διξω
40 πρηγμ οιον ουχ ωρηκας εξ οτου ζωις
Κυδιλλ' ιουσα τον νεωκορον βωσον
ου σοι λεγω αύτη τηι... χωδε χασκευσηι
μα μη τιν ωρην ων λεγω πεποιηται
εστηκε δ εις μ ορευσα καρκινον μεζον

21. την: corrected from τον.
22. εποει: a slip for εποιει.
27. κεινην: originally written κειμενην, but the letters με are cancelled by dots placed above them.
30. Mr. A. S. Murray suggests that the old man here mentioned belongs to the same group as that described in the following lines. In that case we have an old man (presumably leaning on a staff, as usual in reliefs) looking at a boy strangling a χηναλώπηξ. Pliny (*N. H.* xxxiv. 84) mentions a group of a boy strangling a goose by Boethus. This has been taken to be a purely *genre* subject, but if the old man is part of the group he may be taken to represent Asclepius, watching an infant Asclepiad at his feet.

33. χρονωι: corrected from κρονωι.
36. οκως: corrected from οπως.
37. τις αυτην: these letters are almost obliterated, but the visible remains are consistent with this reading, which has been suggested by Mr. Hicks and Mr. Rutherford.
38. ικονεισμα: the ε is added above the line, and so is the s of ... ης.
42. The letters in the lacuna may be ωδε, which is the reading suggested by Mr. Rutherford.
44. καρκινου: the third letter is rather doubtful.

26   ΗΡΩΔΟΥ ΜΙΜΙΑΜΒΟΙ.

             45 ιουσα φημι τον νεωκορον βωσον
                λάιμαστρον ουτ οργη σ[ε] κρηγυην ουτε
                βεβηλος αινῖ πανταχηι δ... κισαι
                μαρτυρομαι Κυδιλλα τον θ[εον] τουτον
                ως εκ με καιτ ου θελουσαν οιδησαι
             50 μαρτυρομαι φιμι ες σε τημ[ερ]ηι κινηι
                εν η το βρεγμα τουτο τωυσυρος κνησηι
                μη πανθ ετοιμως καρδιη βαλοι Κυννοι
COL. 22.   δουλη οτι δουλης δ ωτα νωθριη θλιβι
                αλλ ημερη τε κηπι μεζον ωθιται
             55 αυτη συ μινον η θυρη γαρ ωικται
                κἀνεῖθ ο παστος ουχ οργης φιλη Κυννοι
                οι εργα κοινην ταυτ ερις Αθηναιην
                γλυψαι τα καλα χαιρετω δε δεσποινα
                τον παιδα δη γυμνον ην κνιγω τουτον
             60 ουχ ελκος εξι Κυννα προς γαρ οι κινται
                αις αρκεσοι αθερμα θερμα πηδωσαι
                εν τηι σανισκηι τωργυρευν δε πύραγρον
                ουκ ην ιδη Μυελλος η Παταικισκος
                ο Λαμπριωνος εκβαλευσι τας κουρας
             65 δοκευντες οντως αργυρευν πεποιησθαι
                ο βους δε χο αγων αυτον η θ ομαρτευσα
                χω γρυπος ουτος κω [αν]ασιλλος ανθρωπος

46. κρηγυην: the first two letters are somewhat faint.

49. The metre of this line is defective, and the letters between the α of και and ου are doubtful. Qu. καιτ⟨οι⟩ or καιπ⟨ερ⟩?

50. τημερηι: the supplement is due to Mr. Hicks.

κινηι: at first written κεινηι, but the ε is dotted in order to cancel it.

51. η: corrected from ηι. The two letters before κνησηι are doubtful.

52. βαλοι: there is considerable doubt about this word. An α appears to follow the λ, but is cancelled by a dot above it; and the ο appears to have been re-written.

53. θλιβι: at first written θλιβει, but the ε is dotted in order to cancel it.

57. οι εργα κοινην: or, as Mr. Rutherford suggests, οι εργ ακοιν ην.

59. The metre is defective, but it might be remedied by inserting τον before γυμνον.

61. θερμα has been omitted by inadvertence, and is added above the line in another hand. The first words in this line might also be divided as αι σαρκες οι αθερμα, but the exact meaning is not clear in either case..

62. πυραγρον: after the second ρ another ρ is added above the line, but unnecessarily.

63. Μυελλος: the letters ελ are added above the line.

67. After ουτος the word ουκ has been written and cancelled.

ουχι ζοην βλεπουσιν ημερην παντες
ει μη εδοκουν τι μεζον η γυνη πρησσιν
70 ανηλαλαξ αν μη μ ο βους τι πημηνηι
COL. 23. ουτως επιλοξοι Κυννι τηι ετερηι κουρηι
αληθιναι φιλη γαρ αι Εφεσιου χιρες
ες παντ Απελλεω γραμματ ουδ ερις κινος
ωνθρωπος εν μεν ιδεν εν δ απηρινηθη
75 αλλ ωι επι νουν γενοιτο και θεων ψαυιν
ηπιγεθ ος δ εκινον η εργα τα εκεινου
μη παμφαλησας εκ δικης ορωρηκεν
ποδος κρεμαιτ εκεινος εν γναφεως οικωι
και υμιν ω γυναικες εντελεως τα ιρα
80 και ες λωιον εμβλεποντα μεζονως ου τις
ηρεσατο τον Παιηον ηπερ ουν υμις
ιη ιη Παιηον ευμενης ιης
καλοις επ ιροις ταισδε κι τινες τωνδε
εας οπυιηται τε και γενης ασσον
85 ιη ιη Παιηον ωδε ταυτ ιη
ιη γαρ ω μεγιστε χυγιηι πολληι
ελθοιμεν αυτις μεζον ιρ αγινευσαι
συν ανδρασιν και παισι Κοτταλη καλως
τεμευσα μεμνεο το σκελυδριον δουναι
COL. 24. 90 τωι νεοκορωι τουρνιθος ες τε την τρωγλην
τον πελανον ενθες του δρακοντος ευφημως
και .. αιστα δευσον ταλλα δ οικιης εδρηι
δαισομεθα και επι μη λαθη φεριν αυτη
της υγιιης λωι προσδος η γαρ ιροισιν
95 με[ζ]ων αμαρτιης η υγιη στι της μοιρης

76. τα is added above the line.
77. ορωρηκεν: cf. v. 4, VI. 19, 44.
79. After εντελεως is written an ι, which has been cancelled by a dot above it.
80. μεζονως: the σ is added above the line in another hand.
81. υμις: at first written υμεις, but the ε is cancelled by a dot above it.
83. επιροις: originally written εμπροις.
94. λωι: corrected from δωι.

V.

Ζηλοτυπος

λεγε μοι συ Γαστρων η δ υπερκορης ουτω
ωστ ουκετ αρκι ταμα σοι σκελεα κινιν
αλλ Λμφυταιηι τηι Μενωνος εγκισαι
εγω Λμφυταιην την λεγεις ορωρηκα
5 γυναικα προφασῖς πασαν ημεραν ελκις
Βίτιννα δουλος ιμι χρω ο τι βουλι
και μη το μευ αιμα νυκτα κημερην [πι]νε
οσην δε και την γλασσαν ουτος εσχηκας
Κυδιλλα κου στι Πυρριης καλι μ αυτον
10 τι εστι τουτον δησον αλλ εθ εστηκας
την ιμανηθρην του καδου ταχεως λυσας
Col. 25. ην μη καταικισασα τηι γ οληι χωρηι
παραδιγμα θω μα μη με θηις γυναικ ιναι
ηρ ουχι μαλλον Φρυξ εγω αιτιη τουτων
15 εγῶ ιμι Γαστρων η σε θεισα εν ανθρωποις
αλλ ι τοτ εξημαρτον ου τα νυν ευσαν
μῶραν Βιτινναν ως δοκις εθ ευρησις
φερ ἰς συ δησον την απληγιδ εκδυσας
μη μη Βιτιννα των σε γουνατων δουμαι
20 εκδυθι φημι δι σ οτευνεκ ι δουλος
και τρις υπερ σευ μνας εθηκα γινωισκιν
ως μη καλως γενοιτο τημερηι κινηι
ητις σ εσηγαγ ωδε Πυρριη κλαυσι
ορω σε δηκου παντα μαλλον η δευντα
25 συγσφιγγε τους αγκωνας εκπρισον δησας
Βιτιννα αφες μοι την αμαρτιην ταυτην
ανθρωπος ιμι ημαρτον αλλ επην αυτις
ελης τι δρωντα των συ μη θεληις στιξον

V.
4. λεγεις: corrected from μενων, the scribe having begun to write the name Μενωνος as in the previous line.
9. κου στι: corrected from που μυ
11. του: corrected from τουτου.
12. τηι γ: or τηις.
14. ηρ: the η is corrected from ε.
18. δησον: corrected from δυσον.
26. αμαρτιην: corrected from αμαρτιαν.

ΗΡΩΔΟΥ ΜΙΜΙΑΜΒΟΙ.

```
              προς Αμφυταιην ταυτα μη με πληκτιζευ
COL. 26.  30  μεθ ης αλιν δι και εμον . η ... οψηστρον
              δεδεται καλως σοι μη λαθη λυθις σκεψαι
              αγ αυτον εις το ζητρειον προς Ερμωνα
              και χιλιας μεν ες τον νωτον εγκοψαι
              αυτωι κελευσον χιλιας δε τηι γαστρι
          35  αποκτενεις Βιτιννα μ ουδ ελεγξασα
              ιτ εστ αληθεα πρωτον ειτε και ψευδεα
              α δ αυτος ιπας αρτι τηι ιδιαι γλασσηι
              Βιτινν αφες μοι την αμαρτιην ταυτην
              την σευ χολην γαρ ηθελον κατασβωσαι
          40  εστηκας εμβλεπων συ κουκ αγις αυτον
              οκου λεγω σοι οδῆ Κυδιλλα το ρυγχος
              του παντοερκτεω τουδε και συ μοι Δρηχων
              ηδη φαμαρτι σοι εαν ουτος ηγηται
              δωσις τι δουλη τωι κατηρητωι τουτωι
          45  ρακος καλυψαι την ανωνυμον κερκον
              ως μη δι αγορης γυμνος ων θεωρηται
              το δευτερον σοι Πυρριη παλιν φωνεω
              οκως ερις Ερμωνι χιλιας ωδε
COL. 27.      και χιλιας ωδ εμβαλιν ακηκουκάς
          50  ως ην τι τουτων ων λεγω παραστιξηις
              αυτος συ και ταρχαια και τοκους τισις
              βαδιζε και μη παρα τα Μικκαλης αυτον
              αγ αλλα την ιβιαν ουδ επεμνησθην
              καλι καλι δραμευσα πριν μακρην δουλη
          55  αυτος γενεσθαι Πυρριης ταλας κωφε
              καλι σε μα δοξι τις ουχι συνδουλον
              αυτον σπαραττιν αλλα σηματων φωρα
```

31. μη : corrected from μεθ.
32. αγ αυτον εις το ζητρειον : quoted in Etym. Mag. s. v. ζήτρειον· σημαίνει τὸ τῶν δούλων δεσμωτήριον, ἤγουν τὸν μύλωνα, παρὰ Χίοις καὶ Ἀχαιοῖς.... καὶ παρὰ Ἡροδότῳ (l. Ἡρώδᾳ), "Ἄγε αὐτὸν εἰς τὸ ζήτρειον. ἔστι δὲ χορίαμβον (l. χωλίαμβον) τὸ μέτρον. The corrections were made by Ruhnken (Meineke, Frag. 8).

37. ιπας : an ε is prefixed above the line.
41. οδη : qu. a mistake for ορη?
42. τουδε : corrected from τουτου.
43. φαμαρτι : qu. for (ε)φομαρτ(ε)ι, as suggested by Mr. Hicks?
    σοι εαν : qu. 'φομαρτις οι εαν?
56. συνδουλον : συν is added above the line.

ΗΡΩΔΟΤ ΜΙΜΙΑΜΒΟΙ.

ορηις οκως νυν τουτον εκ βιης ελκις
ες τας αναγκας Πυρριη εμα τουτοις
60 τους δυο Κυδιλλ εποψεθ ημερεων πεντε
παρ Αντιδωρωι τας αχαικας κινας
ας πρων εθηκας τοις σφυροισι τριβοντα
ουτος συ τουτον αυτις ωδ εχων ηκε
δεδεμενον ουτως ωσπερ εξαγις αυτον
65 Κοσιν τ εμοι κελευσον ελθιν τον στικτην
εχοντα ραφιδας και μελαν μιηι δἶ σε

Col. 28. οδωι γενεσθαι ποικιλον κατηρτησθω
ου[τ]ω κατα μυος ωσπερ η Δαου τιμη
μη. ατί αλλα νυν μεν αυτον ουτω σοι
70 [ζω]ιη Βατυλλις κηπιδοις μεν ελθουσαν
ες ανδρος οικον και τεκν αγκαλαις αραις
αφες παραιτευμαι σε την μιαν ταυτην
αμαρτιην Κυδιλλα μη λυπιτε με
η φευξομ εκ της οικιης αφεω τουτον
75 τ[ο]ν επταδουλον και τις ουκ απαντωσα
ες μεν δικαιως το προσωπον εμπτυοι
ο . . ην τυραννον αλλ επειπερ ουκ οιδεν
ανθρωπος ων εωυτον αυτικ ιδησι
εν τωι μετωπω το επιγραμμα εχων τουτο
80 αλλ εστιν ικας και Γερηνι ες πεμπτην
νυν μεν σ αφησω και εχε την χαριν ταυτηι
ην ουδεν ηττον η Βατυλλιδα στεργω
εν τηισι χερσι τηις εμηισι θρεψασα
επεαν δε τοις καμουσιν εγχυτλωσωμεν

Col. 29. 85 αξις τοτ αμ[ε]λι τ[ην] εορτην εξ εορτης

63. αυτις: corrected from αυθις.
69. σοι: originally written σω, but a correction has been made in faint ink.
70. ζωιη: the supplement is due to Mr. Hicks.
74, 75. αφεω τουτον τον επταδουλον: Eustathius (ad Hom. p. 1542, 50) quotes this as from Hipponax, and again (p. 725, 35) refers to the same author for the word επταδουλον. *Cf.* Bergk, Frag. 74 (Meineke, Frag. 79).

Herodas must have borrowed it as a quotation, unless Eustathius made a mistake as to his authority.
77. ο..ην: the visible remains are consistent with reading ουσην.
επειπερ: written επεπειπερ by inadvertence.
85. The supplements in this line are proposed by Mr. Hicks, and are consistent with the visible remains of letters.

VI.

Φι[λ]ιαζ[ο]υσαι η ιδιαζουσαι

καθησο Μητροι τηι γυναικιας ες διφρον
ανασταθεισ[α] παντα δει με προσταττιν
αυτην συ δ ουδεν αν ταλαινα ποιησαις
αυτη απο σαυτης μα λιθος τις ου δουλη
5 εν τηι οικιηι εις αλλα ταλφιτ ην μετρη
τα κριμν αμιθρεις κη τοσουτ αποσταξει
την ημε[ρη]ν ολην σε τονθορυζουσαν
και πρημονωσαν ου φερουσιν οι τοιχοι
νυν αυτον [ε]κμασσις τε και ποις λαμπρον
10 οτ ες τι χρ . . ληστρι θυε μοι ταυτηι
επει σε γε . . αν των εμων εγω χειρεων
φιλη Κοριττοι ταυτ[ο μοι] ζυγον τριβις
κηγω επιβρυχουσα [η]μερην τε και νυκτα
κυων υλακτεω ται[ς] ανωνυμοις ταυταις
15 αλλ ουνεκεν π[ρ]ος σ [ηλθ]ον εκποδων ημιν
φθιρεσθε νω βυστρα ω[τα] μουνον και γλασσαι
τα δ αλλ εορτηι λισσομα[ι σε] μη ψευσηι
COL. 30.   φιλη Κοριττοι τις ποτ ην ο σευ ραψας
τον κοκκινον βαυβωνα κου δ ορωρηκας
20 Μητροι συ κινον Νοσσις ε[ι]χεν ηριννης
τριτημερη νιν μα καλον τι δωρημα
Νοσσις κοθεν λαβουσα διαβαλις ην σοι
ειπω μα τουτους τους γλυκεας φιλη Μητροι
εκ του Κοριττους στοματος ουδεις μη ακουσηι

VI.

1. γυναικιας : apparently the scribe began to write γυναικιδος, but altered the word before reaching the last letter, as the last two letters of γυναικιας are written over δο. The α, however, is not certain, and as there is a dot above it, it may be intended to be cancelled.

2. ανασταθεισα : the last five letters are doubtful, being partially lost in a worm-hole.

5. μετρη : corrected from μετρεω.

6. αμιθρεις : the second letter is doubtful. Cf. l. 98.

10. ληστρι : the λ might be read as an α.

11. χειρεων : corrected from χειρων.

12. τριβις : at first written τριβεις, but the ε is cancelled by a dot above it.

16. ωτα : this supplement is proposed by Mr. Hicks.

18. σευ : the reading is doubtful.

19. κοκκινον : corrected from κονκινον.

ΗΡΩΔΟΥ ΜΙΜΙΑΜΒΟΙ.

25 οσ αν συ λεξηις η Βιτᾶτος Ευβουλη
ε̄δωκεν αυτηι και ειπε μηδεν αισθεσθαι
γ̄υναικες αυτη μη γυνη ποτ εκτριψι
εγω μεν αυτην λιπαρευσαν ηιδεσθην
κηδωκα Μητροι προσθεν η αυτη χρησασθαι
30 η δ ωπερ ευρημ αρπασα δωριται
και ταισι μη δι χαιρετω φιλη πολλα
εουσα τοιη χητερην τιν ανθ ημεων
φιλην αθριτω ταλλα Νοσσιδ[ι] χρ[ησ]θαι
τηι μη δοκεω μεζον μεν η γυν[η] ... ξω
35 λαθοιμι δ αδρηστια χιλιων ευντων
ενα ουκ αν οστις σαπρος εστι προσδοιην

COL. 31. μη δη Κοριττοι την χολην επι ρινος
εχ ευθυς ην τι ρημα μη καλον πευθηι
γυναικος εστι κρηγυης φεριν παντα
40 εγω δε τουτων αιτιη λαλευσ ιμι
πολλα την μεν γλωσσαν εκτεμιν διται
εκεινο δ ου σοι και μαλιστ επεμνησθην
τις εσθ ο ραψας αυτον ι φιλις μ ἶπον
τι μ ενβλεπεις γελωσα νυν ορωρηκας
45 Μητρουν το πρωτον η τι ταβρα σοι ταυτα
ενευχομαι Κοριττι μη μ επιψευσηι
αλλ ιπε τον ραψαντα μα η μοι εν ευχη
Κ̄ερδων ερραψε κοιος ειπε μοι Κερδων
δυ ισι γαρ Κερδωνες ις μεν ο γλαυκος
50 ο Μυρταλινης της Κυλαιθιδος γιτων

30. ωπερ: presumably should be ωσπερ.
   αρπασα: so the MS. for αρπασασα.
33. χρησθαι: the last two letters are added above the line.
34. γυνη ...: over the termination of the line is written a correction, of which the greater part is destroyed; only the letters ικτ (or ικη, qu. δικη?), standing above νν, are legible, with a υ about four letters later.
36. σαπρος: corrected from λεπρος.
   προσδοιην: corrected from προσδωσω.

37-39. Quoted by Stobaeus, *Flor.* 74, 14, as from Ἡρώδου [al. Ῥώδα] Μιμιάμβων (Meineke, Frag. 2). Stobaeus reads κορη τυ for the proper name Κοριττοι, and ρινας for ρινος.
38. καλον: corrected from συφον, which is read in Stobaeus.
41. The metre is defective, but may be remedied by inserting και or η before πολλα.
43. ι: at first written ει, but the ε is cancelled by a dot above it.

ΗΡΩΔΟΥ ΜΙΜΙΑΜΒΟΙ. 33

αλλ ουτος ουδ αν πληκτρον ες λυρην ραψαι
ο δ ετερος εγγυς της συνοικιης οικεων
της Ερμοδωρου την πλατειαν εκβαντι
ην μεν κοτ ην τις αλλα νυν γεγηρακε

Col. 32. 55 τουτωι ... αιθις η μακαριτις εχρητο
μνησθειεν αυτης οιτινες προσηκουσι
ουδετερος αυτων εστιν ως λεγεις Μητροι
αλλ ουτος ουκ οιδ η Χιου τις ηρυθρεων
ηκι φαλακρος μικκος αυτο ερις ιναι

60 Πρηξινον ουδ αν συκον ικασαις συκωι
εχοις αν [ουτ]ω πλην επην λαληι γνωσηι
Κερδων οτεννεκ εστι και ουχι Πρηξινος
κατοικειν δ εργαζετ ενπολεων λαθρη
τους γαρ τελωνας πασα νυν θυρη φρισσει

65 αλλ εργ οκοι εστ εργα της Αθηναιης
αυτης οραν τας χειρας ουχι Κερδωνος
δοξεις .... εν δυο γαρ ηλθ εχων Μητροι
ιδουσα μ.... τωμματ εξεκυμηνα
τα βαλλι ουτως ανδρες ουχι ποιευσι

70 αυται γαρ ..... ορθα κου μονον τουτο
αλλ η μαλακοτης υπνος οι δ ιμαντισκοι
ερι ουχι μ..... ευνοεστερον σκυτεα

Col. 33. γυναικ[ι] διφωσ αλλον ουκ αν ευρ[ο]ις
κως ουν αφηκας τον ετερον [τι] δ ου Μητροι

75 επρηξα κοιην δ ου προσηγαγ[ο]ν πιθουν
αυτωι φιλευσα το φαλακρον κ[α]ταψωσα
γλυκυν πιειν εγχευσα ταταλιζουσα

52. οικεων: the ε is added above the line.
60. ικασαις: there are traces of a dot above the last letter, to cancel it, which is required by the construction.
63. The metre is defective, and perhaps κατοικεων should be read, or else κατ οικιην, as Mr. Rutherford has suggested. A line has been drawn in the margin of the MS. to call attention to the defect.
65. οκοι εστ: the reading is doubtful, especially the letters οι ε.
67. εν: or ειν.
73. This column has been torn apart near the ends of the lines, and in rejoining a letter or part of a letter is sometimes lost. The metre of the first line is defective.
77. ταταλιζουσα: this reading is due to a conjecture by Mr. Hicks. The ζ is not quite certain. For τατα = τεττα, cf. III. 79.

F

ΗΡΩΔΟΥ ΜΙΜΙΑΜΒΟΙ.

```
        το σωμα μουνον ουχι δουσα χρησασθαι
        αλλ ι σε και τουτ ηξιωσ εδει δουναι
     80 εδει γαρ αλλα καιρον ου πρεποντ ιναι
        ηληθεν γαρ η Βιτατος εν μεσωι δουλη
        αυτη γαρ ημεων ημερην τε και νυκτα
        τριβουσα τον ονον σκωριην πεποιηκεν
        οκως τον ωυτης μη τετρωβολο[υ] κοψηι
     85 κως δ ουτος ευρε προς σε την οδον ταυτην
        φιλη Κοριττοι μηδε τουτο με ψευσ[ηι]
        επεμψεν αυτον Αρτεμις η Κανδατ[ο]ς
        του βυρσοδεψεω την στεγην σημηνασα
        δι ει μεν Αρτεμις τι καινον ευρησει
     90 προσω πιευσα την προκυκλιην θαλ . . . . ν
        αλλ ουν τοτ ουχι τους δυ ιχες εκλυσαι
COL. 34. εδει πυθεσ[θ]αι τον ετερον τις η ε[κ]δουσα
        ελιπαρεον ο δ ω[μο]σεν ουκ αν ιπιν μοι
        λεγεις οδον μοι νυν προς Αρτεμιν ιναι
     95 οκως ο Κ[ερ]δ[ω]ν οστις εστιν ιδ[ω ε]γω
        υγιαιν εμ . . . . . . . λαιματ . . χωρει
        ημι . . φ . . . . . . . στι την θυρην κλισον
        αυτ . . υ . . . . το . . . λι καξαμιθρησαι
        αια . . . . . . . εσ . . . αι εισι των τε αιρεων
    100 αυτηι . . . . . . . . ου γαρ αλλα πορθευ . .
        ωρν[υ]θ . . . . . . . . αι κην τρεφηι τις εν κολπωι
```

79. εδει : the second ε is added above the line.

81. ηληθεν : *i.e.* ηλθεν. μεσωι : the termination is doubtful.

84. The reading of this line is due to a suggestion of Mr. Hicks.

87. Κανδατυς : the last three letters are not certain.

90. There is a correction written over the last word of the line, but it is illegible.

92. This column has been very considerably mutilated by worms.

93. ωμοσεν : the restoration is due to Mr. Hicks. ιπιν : at first written ειπειν, but the two ε's are dotted, so as to cancel them. In the margin at the end of this line are the characters α″, referring to an omitted line which has been written in a different hand (a small cursive) at the top of the column. It is not easy to read, but appears to run ταυτηι γαρ και ηγαπησεν μητρωι, in which case the metre is defective.

98. καξαμιθρησαι : the μ and ι are doubtful, being partially lost in a worm-hole.

ΗΡΩΔΟΤ ΜΙΜΙΑΜΒΟΙ. 35

VII.

[Σκυτε]υς

Κερδων αγω [σ]οι τασδε τας ....
των [σ]ων εχις αυτηισιν αξιον δι[ξ]αι
χειρεων νοηρες εργον ου ματην μητοι
εγω φιλω σε ταις γυναιξιν ου θησεις
5 την μεζον εξω [σ]ανιδα Δριμυλω φωνεω
παλιν καθευδις κοπτε Πιστε το ρυγχος
αυτου μεχρις τον υπνον εκχεηι παντα
Col. 35. μαλλον δε την ακαν[θαν] ....
εκ του τραχηλου δησο[ν] ....
10 κινι ταχεως τα γουνα[τ] ....
[τ]ριβιν ψοφευντα νουθ..... [τ]ουτων δε
ν[υ]ν εκ μιν αυτην λε.......... υνις
κ........... τη.......... ψησω
εζ......... πιστ.......... ξας
15 πυ. γιδα μη την ωδ.......... ν
τα χρησιμ εργα τουτ.......... ος
ταχεως ενεγκ ανω.......... ροι
οι εργ εποψεσθ ησυχη........ ον
την αμβαλου[χ]ην οι........ [π]ρωτον
20 Μητροι τελεων αρη........ ων ιχνος
θηεισθε χυμε[ι]ς ω γυ.......... ρνη
ορηθ οπως πεπηγε.......... οις
εξηιτιωται πασα κ.......... ως
τα δ ουχι καλως αλλα πα.......... ς
25 το χρωμα δ ουτως.......... δοιη
Col. 36. .... εριχανασθ επαυρεσθαι
.... οτωι δ ισον χρ[ω]μα

VII.

1. Nearly the whole of this poem has suffered seriously from the papyrus being either destroyed or much rubbed.

3. μητοι: or μητρι, i.e. Μητροι, the proper name.

8. Much of this column has been eaten away by worms.

11. τουτων: the letters ου are dotted, presumably in order to cancel them.

26. The first half of this column has been destroyed by worms.

F 2

```
         .......... οκου δε κηρος ανθησει
         .......... τρις εδωκε Κανδᾶ[τι]
      30 .......... τουτο κητερον χρωμα
         .......... μη πανθ ος εστιν .. α
         ........ τ .......... βαδιζειν
         .......... ουδ οσον ροπην ψευδος
         ........ [Κ]ερδωνι μη βιου ονησις
      35 .......... ων γινοιτο και χαριν προς με
         ........ ρ αλλα μεζονων ηδη
         .......... κερδεων οριγνωνται
         ........ τ αθρρα της τεχνης ημων
         ........ τος δε δειλαιην οιζυν
      40 .......... εων νυκτα κημερην θαλπω
         ........ ον αχρι εσπερης καπτει
         ........ ορθ[ρ]ον ου δοκεω .. σον
COL. 37.   τα μικρων οσ .. η ριθ υπ ..........
           κουπω λεγω τρις και δε[κα] ..... σκω
       45 οτευνεκ ω γυναικες αρ ..........
           οἵ κην υηιζου. τουτ ομο ..........
           φερει ' φερεις τι ταλλα δ ..........ται
           οκως νεοσσο[ι] τας κηχωνασθαι [πα]ντες
           αλλ ου λογων γαρ φασιν η αγορη δειται
       50 χαλκων δε τ[α]υτην .. υμινα .. ανηι Μητρ[οι]
           το ζευγος ετερον χατε[ρ]ον μαλ εξοισει
           εστ αν ...... πισθητε ... ετει ψευδεα
           Κερδωνα τας μ ....... ουκ ιδας πασας
           ενεγκε Πιστε ........ νη θεισα
       55 υμεας απελθιν ω γυναικες εις οικον
           θησεσθε δ υμ .... νεα τ[α]υτα παντοια
           Σικωνια Λμβρακιδια νο[σσ]ιδες λειαι
           ψιντακαια κανναβισκα βαυκιδ[ες] βλαυττια
```

44. λεγω: or μ.τω.
45. οτευνεκ: corrected from οτουνεκ.
48. οκως: corrected from ορσως.
49. λογων: the first two letters are doubtful.
56. The readings in the latter part of this line are doubtful.
57. Σικωνια: the ω is written above the line as an addition.
58. βλαυττια: the second τ is added above the line.

ΗΡΩΔΟΥ ΜΙΜΙΑΜΒΟΙ.   57

           Ιωνικ αμφισφαιρα νυκ[τ]ιπηδ[ηκ]ες
     60 ακροσφυρια καρκινια σαμβαλ Αρ[γ]εια
           κοκκιδες εφηβοι διαβαθρα ων ερα θ[υ]μος
COL. 38. υμεων εκαστης ειπατ ως αν αισθοισθε
           σκυτεα γυναικες και κυνες τι βρωζουσιν
           κοσου χρειζεις κιν ο προσθεν ηαρας
     65 απεμπολη ζευγος αλλα μη βροντεων
           αυτος συ τρεψηις μεζον εις φυγην ημεας
           αυτη συ και τιμησον ει θελις αυτο
           και στησον ης κοτ εστιν αξιον τιμης
           ι τουτο .... γαρ ους ερηι δι ων....
     70 δευτε ων γυναι τωληθες ην θεληις εργον
           ερις τι ναι μα τηνδε την τεφρην κορσην
           εφ ης αλω...ξ ν..σι....ε........
           ταχ αλφιτηρον ε..α...α κινευσι
           Ερμη τε κερδεων και συ κερδιη πιθοι
     75 ως ην τι μη νυν ημιν ες βολον κυρσηι
           ουκ οιδ οκως αμινον η χυτρη πρηξι
           τι τονθορυζεις κουκ ελευθερηι γλασσηι
           τον τιμον οστις εστιν εξεδιφησας
           γυναι μιης [μνης] εστιν αξιον τουτο
COL. 39. 80 το ζευγος η ανω σ η κατω βλεπιν χαλκου
           ρινημ ο δη κοτ εστι της Αθηναιης
           ωνευμενης αυτης αν ουκ αποσταξαι
           μαλ εικοτως σευ το στεγυλλιον Κερδων
           πεπληθε δαψιλεων τε και καλων εργων
     85 φυλασσε κα..ας αυτα τηι γαρ ικοστηι
           του Ταυρεωνος η Κατη γαμον ποιι
           [τ]ης Αρ[τα]κηνῆς κυποδυματων χρειη
           ταχ ουν ταλη .... υσι συν τυχηι προς σε

64. ηαρας : so, apparently, for ηειρας.

65. The metre is defective; possibly it should be restored by inserting το before ζευγος.

73. A stroke is drawn in the margin, apparently to denote that some correction is needed in this line.

77. τονθορυζεις : the ς is added above the line.

87. της Αρτακηνης : the reading is doubtful, except the last four letters.

88. A stroke is drawn in the margin, indicating some corruption.

```
            μαλλον δε παντως αλλα θυλακον ραψαι
        90  τας μνεας οκως σοι μη αι γαλαι διοισουσι
            ην τ η κατελθηι μνης ελασσον ουκ οισι
            ην τ ηι Αρτακηνη προς ταδ ει θελις σκεπτευ
            ου σοι διδωσιν η αγαθη τυχη Κ[ε]ρδων
            ψαυσαι ποδισκων ων ποθοι τε χηρωτες
        95  ψανουσιν αλλ ισκνυσα και κακη λωβη
            ωστ εκ μεν ημεων . . . λεοσεω πρηξις
            ταυτηι δε δωσις κε[ι]νο το ετερον ζευγος
Col. 10.    κοσου παλιν πρημηνον αξιαν φω[ν]ην
            σεωτου στατηρας πεντε ναι μα θεους φο[ι]ται
       100  η ψαλτρι ετηρις ημερην πασαν
            λαβιν ανωγουσ αλλ εγω μιν [εχθα]ιρω
            κην τεσσαρας μοι δαρεικους υποσχηται
            οτουνεκεν μευ την γυναικα τωθαζει
            κακοισι δεινοις ει . . . . . . . . . χρειη
       105  φερ ευλαβου των τριω . . . . . . . δουναι
            και ταυτ αυτα και ταυτ . . . . . . . . . . . ικων
            εκητι Μητρους της δ . . . . . . . . . ει . . .
            . . ναι το μ ελασαι σαν . . . . . . . . . . .
            εοντ αληθινον εσθ εουσαν αττη . . .
       110  εχις γαρ ουχι γλασσαν ηδηνης δη ελθιν
```

89. There is a hole in the MS. between the α and ν of παντως, and between the κ and ω of οκως in the following line; but it must have been there when the papyrus was originally used, as the metre is complete.

91. ουκ: corrected from ουχ.

96. ημεων: the following letters appear to be λιπλευσεω, the last six appearing to be certain; but there must be some corruption and this is indicated by a stroke in the margin opposite the line.

99. σεωτου was originally omitted in the text, but is added in the margin. At the top of the column is written σεωτου στατηρ⁰ᵘ.

100. A word must have been accidentally omitted from this line. The terminations of all the lines in this column are much obliterated, but there is no trace of any word having been written after πασαν; moreover πασαν, though admissible, would not be usual for the penultimate foot of the line. Probably, as Mr. Hicks suggests, ετημις is the termination of a proper name.

104. δεινοις: corrected from δεννοις, but probably wrongly. A piece of the papyrus is lost, which causes a lacuna in this and the four following lines. The piece which contains the final letters of these lines, too, is rubbed, and the reading χρειη is not certain.

106. ταυτ αυτα: presumably only a dittography for ταυτα.

110. ελθιν: the reading is doubtful. There appears to be a stroke in the margin opposite this line, so there is probably some corruption in it.

ΗΡΩΔΟΥ ΜΙΜΙΑΜΒΟΙ.

αθεων εκινος ου μακρην α.........
οτεω συ χιλεα νυκτα κημερην οι....
φερ ωδε τον ποδισκον εισιν ος θω....
παξ· μητε προσθηις μητ απ ουν ελη μηδεν
115 τα καλα παντα της καληισιν αρμοζι
Col. 41. αυτην ερις το πελμα την Αθηναιην
τεμιν δος αυτη και συ τον ποδα ψωρη
αρηρεν οπλη βους ο λακτισας υμας
ει τις πρ[ο]ς ιχνος ηκονησε την σμιλην
120 ουκ αν μα την Κερδωνος εστιην ουτω
τουργον σαφεως εκειτ αν ως σαφως κιται
αυτη συ δωσις επτα δαρικους τουδε
η μεζον ιππου προς θυρην κιχλιζουσα
γυναικες ην εχητε κητερων χρειην
125 η σαμβαλισκων η ακατοικιην ελκιν
ειθ ισθε την μοι δουλ[ην] ωδε πεμπιν
συ δ ηκε Μητροι προς με τηι ενατηι παντως
οκως λαβης καρκινια την γαρ ουν βαιτην
θαλπουσαν ευδειν δολιφρονουντα και ραπτιν

VIII.

Ενυπνιον

α στηθι δουλη ψυλλα μεχρι τεο κισηι
ρεγχουσα την δε χοιρον ανονη δρυπτι
η προσμενις συ μεχρις ευ ηλιος θαλψι

114. ελη: qu. ελης? The writing is faint, but there does not seem to be room for the necessary letters.
115. της: the ι is added above the line.
116. It is the right-hand half of this column that is contained on the fragment seen by Professor Sayce (cf. Introduction, p. 6). Professor Sayce had, however, only time to make a hasty copy, and his text consequently requires some corrections.
119. την σμιλην: the top portions of the letters την σ are lost.
126. πεμπιν: corrected from πεμπετε, but the metre remains defective. Probably a compound of πεμπειν should be read. A stroke in the margin calls attention to the corruption.
129. δολιφρονουντα: or δυνφρονουντα, which certainly seems to be what the scribe actually wrote.

VIII.

3. θαλψι: corrected from θαλψηι.

APPENDIX.

THE FRAGMENTS OF HERODAS.

(The order is that of Meineke, but the numbers in the 3rd edition of Bergk's *Poetae Lyrici Graeci* are given in brackets.)

1 (3).

Stobaeus, *Flor.* 78, 6, Ἡρώδου Μιμιάμβων.

ἢ χαλκέην μοι μυῖαν ἢ κύθρην παίζει,
ἢ τῇσι μηλάνθῃσιν ἄμματ' ἐξάπτων
τοῦ κεσκίου μοι τὸν γέροντα λωβῆται.

Line 2 : vulgo ἢ ταῖσι μηλολόνθῃς : codd. ἐν ταῖσι μηλάνθυσιν.

2 (4).

Cf. VI. 37-39.

3 (5).

Stobaeus, *Flor.* 98, 28, Ἡρώδα Μιμιάμβων.

ὡς οἰκίην οὐκ ἔστιν εὐμαρέως εὑρεῖν,
ἄνευ κακῶν ζώουσαν· ὃς δ' ἔχει μεῖον,
τοῦτόν τι μεῖζον τουτέρου δόκει πρήσσειν.

Line 3 : libri τούτου . . . δοκεῖ.

4 (6).

Cf. I. 15, 16.

5 (1).

Stobaeus, *Flor.* 116, 21, Ἡρώδου ἐν Μολπεινοῦ.

ἐπὴν τὸν ἑξηκοστὸν ἥλιον κάμψῃς,
ὦ Γρύλλε, Γρύλλε, θνῆσκε καὶ τέφρη γίνευ,

ΗΡΩΔΟΤ ΜΙΜΙΑΜΒΟΙ.

ὡς τυφλὸς οὐπέκεινα τοῦ βίου καμπτήρ·
ἤδη γὰρ αὐγὴ τῆς ζόης ἀπήμβλυνται.

Line 3 : libri ὁ ὑπὲρ κεῖνο.
Line 4 : libri αὕτη τῆς ζωῆς ἀπήμβλυτο. This line is separated from the rest in Stobaeus (116, 22), and was first joined with them by Salmasius.

6 (7).
Cf. I. 67, 68.

7 (2).
Athenaeus, III. 86 b, Ἡρώνδας ἐν Συνεργαζομέναις.
προσφὺς ὅκως τις χοιράδων ἀναρίτης.

8 (8).
Cf. V. 32.

9 (9).
Cf. III. 10.

10 (10).
Schol. Nicand. Ther. 377, καὶ Ἡρώδης ὁμοίως καὶ ἐν ἡμιάμβοις [καὶ ἐν ἡμιάμβοις om. Schneidewin] ἐν τῷ ἐπιγραφομένῳ [al. περιγραφομένῳ vel ὑπογραφομένῳ] Ὕπνῳ [al. ὕμνῳ].

φεύγωμεν ἐκ προσώπου,
μή σ' ἐκπερῶν ὁ πρέσβυς
οὐλῇ κατευθὺ [κρατὸς]
βατηρίῃ κολάψῃ.

Line 3 : Bergk κατιθύ.
Line 4 : libri καλύψῃ.

ΥΠΕΡΕΙΔΟΥ (?) ΚΑΤΑ ΦΙΛΙΠΠΙΔΟΥ.

PAPYRUS CXXXIV.

THE fragment of an oration which follows is written on a roll of papyrus which also contained the third of the epistles attributed to Demosthenes. The papyrus is imperfect at both ends, the first part of the oration and the last of the epistle being alike lost. The remaining portion of the oration is, moreover, somewhat mutilated. The last nine columns of it remain, with several detached fragments belonging to the earlier portion of the work, none of which, however, contains a complete line. The texts of the larger of these are given below. The continuous portion of papyrus on which the oration is written measures 1 ft. 7¼ in. in length, and 9¼ in. in height. There is a margin of about 1½ in. at the top, and nearly 2 in. at the bottom, and the columns are separated by a space of about a quarter of an inch. The columns are narrow, measuring barely 1¾ in. in breadth, and containing from 16 to 19 (generally 17) letters in a line. There are 26 to 28 lines in each column. The columns lean markedly to the right, as is often the case in papyri of early date. The writing is a small and very neat uncial, not unlike that of the MS. which contains the orations of Hyperides against Demosthenes and on behalf of Lycophron and Euxenippus (Brit. Mus. Papp. CVIII. and CXV.), but somewhat smaller and more delicate even than that. The most peculiarly formed character in it is the A, which resembles the Δ, the cross stroke being carried across the left limb and forming a loop with the bottom of the latter. The left limb and the cross stroke are, in fact, written conjointly, by one action of the pen, much like the ordinary modern way of writing a minuscule α, and the right limb joins the top of the letter to the cross stroke. A similarly-formed α occurs in some of the Herculaneum papyri. Ligatures between the letters are frequent and strongly marked. No abbreviations are employed, but the character 7 (or more rarely =) is used to fill up a superfluous space at the end of a line. A horizontal or a circumflex stroke drawn below the beginning of a line denotes a pause in the sense in the course of it; and a larger pause is indicated by leaving a blank space, equivalent to one or two letters. There are

ΔΑ ΟΝ ΟΝ ΔΕΔΩΚΕΝ
ΠΕΙΤΑ ΔΕ ΩΣ ΠΕΡ ΠΙΣΤΩΝ
ΤΕ ΚΑΙ ΜΑΡΤΥΡΙΩΝ ΛΗ
ΛΟΙΚΟΤΩΝ ΔΕ ΚΑΙ ΤΑ ΤΕΥ
ΔΙΕΣΤΟΡΗΤΟΝ ΑΠΑ ΜΑΡ
ΤΥΡΩΝ ΑΠΑΣΙΝ ΑΝΤΟΜΑ
ΣΕΝ ΩΝ ΤΑ ΙΝΑ ΜΗΔΕΝΙ
... ΛΑΣΙΝ ΩΝ ΗΤΟ ΥΜΕ
ΤΕΡΟ ΙΟΥΔΗΣ Θ ΑΙΤΙΟΝ
ΤΗΝ ΩΜΟΤΗΑΝ ΑΛΛΑ
ΤΗ ΔΙΑΜΑΧΗ ΤΑΥΤΗ
ΠΑΙΤΑ ΓΕ ΥΔΗ ΜΑΡΤΥΡΩΝ
ΟΥΤΩ ΚΑΙ ΤΟΙΣ ΠΛΗΚΟΥΣΙ
ΠΑΡΑΙΤΕΙΣΘΩΣ ΕΣΤΙΝ
ΜΗ ΚΕ ΠΡΑΞΕΙΝ ΕΙΔΕ
ΔΗΛΑ ΩΣ ΕΣΤΙΝ ΟΤΙ ΜΗ
ΟΥΤΙΝΩΣ ΕΝ ΤΕ ΛΑΤΟΥΙ
ΠΟΙΟΥΝΤΩΝ ΤΩΣ ΤΟΥ ΚΑΙ
ΤΩΣ ΤΩΝ ΤΟΙΟΥΤΩΝ ΑΣΙ...
... ΑΛΛΑ ΤΕΙΜΩΡΙΑΣ
ΝΑΛΩΝ Η ΠΡΟΣ ΑΛΕΝΗ
ΤΟΥΤΑΝ ΤΩΝ ΑΥΤΟΣ
...ΤΕΗ ΤΕΙ ΜΑΡΤΥ ΛΟΓΙΑ
...ΕΗΠΑΛΑΙ ΑΠΟ ΥΜΙΝ
ΛΑΘΕΝΩΝ ΥΠ... ΤΙΗΑ
ΤΩ ΠΑΙ ΔΙΩΝ ... ΑΦ
ΣΩΝ ΤΕ ΛΑΙ ΔΕ ΜΝΗΜ

ΜΕΛΙΝΗ ΔΙΕΥ ΩΝ ΚΑΙ ΚΩΝ
ΝΟ ΜΩΝ ΑΚΟΥΤΑΝΤΕΣ
ΑΛΛΑ ΤΙΝ ΩΣ ΚΩΛΙΕΝΩΝ
ΤΑ ΤΕΛΙΚΑ ΝΑ ΚΑΙ ΤΑ ΣΩ ΦΕ
ΡΟΝΤΑ ΥΜΕΙΝ ΑΥΤΟΙΣ Η
ΦΙΣΕΣΘΕ

a very few corrections, in two cases apparently in a different hand, employing a differently-formed α, which resembles that used in the other Hyperides MS. mentioned above (*i.e.*, a loop on the left joining a diagonal stroke on the right). In date the MS. must be placed very early, apparently before the other MS. of Hyperides (1st or 2nd cent. B.C.), and perhaps in the 2nd cent. B.C.

No author's name is given in the MS., and it can only be supplied from internal evidence. The speech is one delivered by the prosecutor in a γραφὴ παρανόμων, and as in the course of it (l. 92) he addresses one Philippides by name, it may be presumed that the latter was the defendant [1]. The proposal which gave rise to the prosecution was a motion to award a crown to certain πρόεδροι on account of their uprightness towards the people of Athens, and because they had executed their office in accordance with the laws (δικαιοσύνης τε τῆς εἰς τὸν δῆμον τὸν Ἀθηναίων, καὶ διότι κατὰ τοὺς νόμους προηδρεύκασιν, ll. 86–90). It is evident that there is more in such a proposal as this than meets the ear. It cannot have been usual to vote crowns to the πρόεδροι whenever they did not act illegally, though Aeschines (*in Ctes.* § 3, p. 54) indicates that corrupt practices were tolerably frequent among them; and the gist of the proposal evidently lay in the reference to some action of theirs in putting an important motion of doubtful legality to the vote. The prosecutor declares that he has proved that their action was illegal, and no doubt the real question at issue was the merits of a certain policy with which the motion was connected, and of the politicians with whom it was identified. As in the great case of the Crown, a political battle was fought on a legal issue. As to the sides represented by each party there is no doubt. The prosecutor attacks his opponents in the various terms which we are accustomed to find in the speeches of Demosthenes against Aeschines. They are the men who have always associated with the enemies of Athens—with the Lacedaemonians when they were strong, though their interest in them lapsed when they ceased to be a danger to Athens (ll. 3–12), and with 'the tyrants' in later times (ll. 153–155). They have rejoiced over the disasters that have befallen the city (ll. 139–143). They have always been on the look-out for occasions on which they could do a mischief to the democracy (ll. 125–134).

---

[1] It should also be mentioned that in l. 22 another person is apparently addressed in the vocative, who seems to be Democrates of Aphidna, an obscure politician who is mentioned by Aeschines and elsewhere. The passage is mutilated, and therefore both the name and the bearing of it are uncertain: but from the way in which Democrates has been introduced just before (l. 13) with the name of his deme, as though he was being then mentioned for the first time, it does not seem probable that he was the defendant in the case.

ΥΠΕΡΕΙΔΟΥ (?) ΚΑΤΑ ΦΙΛΙΠΠΙΔΟΥ.

In all this we recognise the tone of an orator of the anti-Macedonian party attacking, after the disaster of Chaeronea, one of the members of the party which had been, or was accused of being, hand in glove with Philip. The evidence on which the particular orator can be identified is slight, but perhaps sufficient. The name of the defendant is, as has been stated above, Philippides[1]; and it is known that a politician of this name was the subject of attack in one of the speeches of Hyperides. The mention of this fact occurs in Athenaeus, and runs as follows:—λεπτὸς δ' ἦν καὶ Φιλιππίδης, καθ' οὗ λόγος ἐστὶν Ὑπερείδῃ τῷ ῥήτορι λέγων αὐτὸν ἕνα τῶν πολιτευομένων εἶναι. ἦν δ' εὐτελὴς τὸ σῶμα διὰ λεπτότητα, ὥς ὁ Ὑπερείδης ἔφη (Athen. XII, p. 552 D; cf. Aelian, Var. Hist. X. 6). This λεπτότης was proverbial, as appears from the phrase Φιλιππίδου λεπτότερον in the comic poet Alexis (Athen. VI, p. 230 B; XI, 502 F). Nothing more is known with certainty of this Philippides. A person of the name, belonging to the deme Pacania, is called as a witness in the speech (attributed to Demosthenes) against Theocrines (Or. 58, § 33, p. 1332), and the same name recurs in that deme in an inscription of 299–298 B.C. (C. I. A. ii. 297)[2]. The Philippides of the speech against Theocrines is probably identical with the person of that name who is twice mentioned by Demosthenes in his speech against Meidias (Or. 21, §§ 208, 215, pp. 581, 583); but as he is there described as a man of great wealth, who had performed the functions of a trierarch (cf. C. I. A. ii. 795, where he appears as a syntrierarch of Demosthenes), it is hardly probable that he is the same as the Philippides whose εὐτέλεια is derided by Hyperides. We are, therefore, left with the information given by Athenaeus, which, so far as it describes him as a politician of the opposite party to Hyperides, is in complete accordance with the present oration. The actual passage cited by Athenaeus does not occur in the fragment before us; but this is not surprising, as it is evident that it belonged to that part of the speech in which Hyperides, following the ordinary precedents of the Athenian courts of law, entertained the jury with witticisms on the personal peculiarities and moral obliquities of his opponent. This section is not contained in our fragment, and therefore absolute proof is wanting that this is the oration from which the quotation in Athenaeus was taken; but there appears to be no other known work to which it has an equal claim to be referred.

---

[1] It is true that there is a lacuna in the MS. between the Φ and the first π, but the space is just sufficient for the three characters ιλι, while it would not hold the ειδι necessary to make the name Pheidippides, which is the only other possible. Moreover Philippides is known as a politician in this period, while a Pheidippides is not.

[2] Cf. Koehler (Hermes V. 347 ff.) for information concerning this Philippides and his family.

The part of the oration which has been preserved is not that which would have been the most valuable. The earlier part would have contained a discussion of some of the political crises of the age of Hyperides, which might have added something to our knowledge of the history of the period. The present fragment opens with a denunciation of the defendant in somewhat general terms, and then passes almost immediately (l. 46) to a final summary of the case and of the issue before the jury. In this summary specific details are naturally out of place, and we therefore cannot be said to acquire much definite increase of historical knowledge. Still, any addition to our stock of classical literature is to be welcomed, and in this case we gain a not inconsiderable specimen of the style and language of the orator who, second only to Demosthenes in his own day (proximus huic, longo sed proximus intervallo), was apparently hopelessly and entirely lost to the knowledge of the modern world, until, less than half a century ago, he began to be given back to us from the tombs of Egypt.

Dr. J. E. Sandys has very kindly read through the proofs of this fragment, and has suggested several corrections and improvements. In particular, the supplements of the lacunas in col. 1, lines 12 to 20, are due to him. Professor Jebb has also given the sheets the benefit of his revision. The dots which mark lacunas indicate the number of letters which appear to be missing; but where both the beginnings and ends of lines are lost, as in col. 1, it is very difficult to be certain as to the exact number, and the slope of the columns and the somewhat uneven length of the lines increase the difficulty.

The autotype plate represents the last column and a quarter of the text, showing the conclusion of the oration.

Col. 1. κατηγορίας ποιοῦνται,
καὶ φανερὸν ποιοῦσιν
ὅτι οὐδὲ τότε φίλοι ὄν-
τες Λακεδαιμονίων ὑ-
5 πὲρ ἐκείνων ἔλεγον,
ἀλλὰ τὴν πόλιν μισοῦν-
τες καὶ τοὺς ἰσχύοντας ἅ-
[μα] καθ' ὑμῶν θεραπεύ-
οντες. ἐπεὶ δὲ νῦν ἡ
10 [ἐκ]είνων δύναμις ἐ[ἰ]ς
[μι]κρὸν μετέστη, τό [τε]
[κο]λακεύειν προεῖν[το καὶ]
[δὴ] καὶ Δημοκράτη[ς το]-
[ύ]τοις ὁ Ἀφιδναῖος...
15 [συγ]καθήμενος η α...
[καθ]ιστὰς γελωτοπ[οιεῖν]
[ἐπὶ] τοῖς τῆς πόλεω[ς ἀτ]-
[υχ]ήμασιν καὶ λό[γους]
[πλάττ]ειν μεθ' ἡμέρ[αν]

1. ποιοῦνται: the final letter is written above the line.

3. τότε: this must refer to some period during the Spartan supremacy when there was enmity between Sparta and Athens. The most probable time is during the war which followed on the liberation of Thebes (378-374 B.C.). It seems to be going too far back to refer it to the time of the Corinthian war.

8. θεραπεύοντες: written εθεραπευοντες originally, but the first ε is cancelled by a dot placed above it.

11. μετέστη: MS. μετεστηι.

13. Δημοκράτης ὁ Ἀφιδναῖος: this person is mentioned in Aesch. *De Fals. Leg.* p. 30, as a member of the βουλή, and as moving to summon the envoy Aristodemus to give an account of his embassy to Macedon. He is also referred to in Isaeus, *De Philoctemonis Hereditate*, p. 58 (*Or.* 6, 22), Arist. *Rhet.* iii. 4. 3, Plutarch, *Praec. reip. ger.* c. 7, 6, Stob. *Flor.* 13, 30, 22, 43, Curt. vi. 5, 9 (though his deme is only mentioned in the first of these passages); but nothing seems to be known about him. The *Dictionary of Classical Biography* identifies him with the Democrates mentioned in the (probably spurious) ψηφίσματα in Demosthenes, *De Corona*, pp. 235, 291, whose deme is there given as Phlya.

16. γελωτοποιεῖν: the MS. has an α between the τ and ο, but there are faint traces of a dot above it, intended to cancel it. Some such verb as εἰώθει, or (as Dr. Sandys suggests) ἐτόλμα, is needed in l. 14 to account for this infinitive.

ΥΠΕΡΕΙΔΟΥ (?) ΚΑΤΑ ΦΙΛΙΠΠΙΔΟΥ.

20 .....ραι, εἰς ἑσπέρα[ν δὲ]
......πων ὡς ὑμ[ᾶς] .
......καίτοι ὦ Δημ[ό]-
[κρατες].. νωι σοὶ οὐκ..
.......ο τοῦ δήμου
25 ....[ο]ὐδὲν διὰ τι..
.......ὑμεῖς οὐ πα[ρ᾽ ἑ]-

COL. 2. τέρου σ᾽ ἔδει μαθεῖν ὅτι ὁ
δῆμος χάριτας ἀποδί-
δωσιν τοῖς εὐεργέταις
30 ἀλλὰ παρὰ σαυτοῦ· α[ὐ]τὸς
γὰρ ὑπὲρ ὧν ἔτερο[ι] εὐ-
εργέτησαν νῦν τὰς [τ]ι-
μὰς κομίζει[ς]. ἔπε[ι]θ᾽ ὅ-
τι ἐν νόμῳ γράψας [ὁ] δῆ-
35 μος ἀπεῖπεν μήτε [λέ]-
γειν ἐξεῖναι [μηδενὶ] κα-
κῶς Ἁρμόδι[ον] καὶ Ἀρ[ισ]-
τογείτονα μήτ᾽ ᾆσα[ι ἐ]-
πὶ τὰ κακίονα . ἦ κ[αὶ]
40 δεινόν ἐστιν [ε]ἰ το[ὺς]
μὲν σοὺς προγόνους =
[ὁ] δῆμος οὐδὲ μεθυσθέν-
[τ]ι ᾤετο δεῖν ἐξεῖναι κα-
[κ]ῶς εἰπεῖν, σὺ δὲ νήφω[ν]

20. Dr. Sandys suggests [ἐν ἀγο]ρᾷ.

21. ......πων: or ......σων.

32. τιμάς: MS. τειμης.

35. ἀπεῖπεν: this law does not appear to be mentioned elsewhere. The orator here refers to it merely to make a rhetorical point. He is still addressing Democrates, who was of the deme of Aphidna, to which Harmodius belonged (Pape, *Worterbuch der griech. Eigennamen*, ed. Benseler), and in which (as appears from C. I. A. ii. 804, l. 165) the name Harmodius was still preserved in 334-333 B.C.; and Hyperides asks if it is reasonable that his ancestors should be protected from evil-speaking even on the part of drunkards, while he himself deliberately speaks evil of the whole people of Athens. *Cf.* Aesch. *in Timarch.*, §§ 132-140, pp. 18, 19.

38, 39. ᾆσαι ἐπί: this supplement, with the reading of the MS. on which it depends, is due to Prof. Jebb and Dr. Sandys. It is possible that τἀπί should be read for ἐπί, which would avoid the hiatus.

39. κακίονα: MS. κακειονα.

43. ᾤετο: MS. ωετο.

ΤΠΕΡΕΙΔΟΤ (?) ΚΑΤΑ ΦΙΛΙΠΠΙΔΟΤ.

45 [τ]ὸν δῆμον κακ[ῶς] λέγεις.
[βρ]αχέα δ' ἔτι πρὸς [ὑ]μᾶς εἰ-
[π]ών, ὦ ἄνδρες δικ[α]στα[ί],
[καὶ] ἀναλογισάμενος, κα-
[ταβ]ήσομαι. γραφὴ πα-
50 [ρα]νόμων ἐστὶν ὑπὲρ
[ἧς τ]ὴν ψῆφον μέλλετε
[οἴσ]ειν. τὸ δὲ ψήφισμα

COL. 3. τὸ κρινόμενον ἔπαινος
προέδρων. ὅτι δὲ προσ-
55 ήκει τοὺς προέδρους
κατὰ τοὺς νόμους προε-
δρεύειν, οὗτοι δὲ παρὰ τοὺς νόμους προηδρεύκασιν,
αὐτῶν τῶν νόμων ἠ-
60 κούετε ἀναγινωσκο-
μένων. τὸ λοιπὸν ἤ-
δη ἐστὶν παρ' ὑμῖν· δεί-
ξετε γὰρ πότερα τοὺς
παράνομα γράφοντας
65 τ[ιμω]ρήσεσθε, ἢ τὰς τοῖς
εὐε[ργέ]ταις ἀποδεδειγμέ-
νας [τι]μὰς ταύτας δώσε-
τε [το]ῖς ἐναντία τοῖς νό-
μοι[ς πρ]οεδρεύουσιν, καὶ
70 ταῦτα ὀμωμοκότες κα-
τὰ τοὺς νόμους ψηφιεῖσ-
[θ]αι. ἀλλὰ μὴν οὐδ' ἐξα-
πατηθῆναι ὑμῖν ἔνεσ-
[τι]ν ὑπὸ τοῦ λόγου αὐ-
75 τῶν, ἂν φῶσιν ἀναγκαῖ-

45. λέγεις : MS. λεγις.
53. κρινόμενον : MS. κρεινομενον.
57. οὗτοι δέ : these words are added above the line.
60. ἀναγινωσκομένων : MS. αναγεινωσκομενων.
62. ὑμῖν : MS. υμειν.
65. τιμωρήσεσθε : MS. τειμωρησεσθε.
67. δώσετε : corrected in the MS. from σωσετε.
73. ὑμῖν : MS. υμειν.
74. λόγου : the λ and γ are written as corrections, apparently of τ and τ.

ΥΠΕΡΕΙΔΟΥ (?) ΚΑΤΑ ΦΙΛΙΠΠΙΔΟΥ.

         α ε[ἶ]να[ι τῷ] δήμῳ τὰ πε-
         ρὶ [τ]ῶν τ[ιμ]ῶν ψηφίζεσ-
         θα[ι]· το[ὺς γ]ὰρ προέδρους
Col. 4. οὐκ ἔνεστιν εἰπεῖν
   80 ὡς ἀνάγκη τις ἦν στεφα-
      νῶσαι. πρὸ[ς δ]ὲ τούτοις
      αὐτὸς ἡμῖν [οὗτ]ος ῥᾳδί-
      αν πεποίηκ[εν] τὴν γνῶ-
      σιν· ἔγραψεν γ[ὰρ] ὧν ἕνε-
   85 κα ἐστεφάνω[σε]ν τοὺς ⋆
      προέδρους, δι[κα]ιοσύνης
      τε τῆς εἰς τὸν δ[ῆμ]ον τὸν
      Ἀθηναίων κα[ὶ δι]ότι κα-
      τὰ τοὺς νόμο[υς π]ροηδρεύ-
   90 κασιν. ἐπὶ δ[ὲ τ]αῦτ' ἄγε 7
      τ' αὐτὸν ἀπολο[γη]σόμε-
      νον, καὶ σύ, ὦ Φ[ιλι]ππίδη,
      δείξας ἀληθῆ εἶ[να]ι τὰ πε-
      ρὶ τῶν προέδρ[ων], ἃ δ' ὑπέ-
   95 θου ἐν τῷ ψηφ[ίσ]ματι ἀ-
      πόφευγε. εἰ δ' ο[ἴει] κορδα-
      κίζων καὶ γελ[ωτ]οποι-
      ῶν, ὅπερ ποι[εῖν] εἴωθας,
      ἐπὶ τῶν δικαστ[ηρ]ίων
  100 ἀποφεύξεσθαι, ... ης
      .... παρὰ τούτω[ν] σ 7
      υγγνώμην ἦ ε .... ι
      να παρὰ τὸ δίκαι[ον] .. τρ

79. Before εἰπεῖν the word ὡς has been written in error, but has been cancelled by dots placed above it.

85. At the end of the line is the character ⋆, to fill up a blank space. The same sign is used elsewhere in this papyrus, but without the surrounding dots.

90. The υ of ταῦτ' is added above the line.

92. καὶ σύ κ.τ.λ.: the construction of the following sentence appears to be imperfect, and perhaps δεῖξον should be substituted for δείξας.

98. εἴωθας: MS. ειωθες.

101. The line concludes with the character 7, in spite of the extraordinary division of the word συγγνώμην which this necessitates.

102. ε .... ινα: possibly ἐλεόν τινα, as sug-

..ειν. πολλοῦ γε δ[εῖ γ]ὰρ
Col. 5. 105 ἀπέθου σαυτῷ εὔνοιαν
παρὰ τῷ δήμῳ· ἀλλ' ἑτέ-
ρωθι, οὐδὲ τοὺς σῶσαί σε
δυναμένους ᾤου δεῖν
κολακεύειν, ἀλλὰ τοὺς τῷ
110 δήμῳ φοβεροὺς ὄντας.
καὶ ἓν μὲν σῶμα ἀθάνα=
τον ὑπ[είλη]φας ἔσεσθαι, πόλεως δὲ τηλικαύτης θάνα-
τον κατέγνως· οὐδ' ἐκεῖνο
115 συνιδών, ὅτι τῶν μὲν τυ-
ράννων οὐδεὶς πώποτε
τελευτήσας ἀνεβίωσεν, =
πόλεις δὲ πολλαὶ ἄρδην ἀν-
αιρεθεῖσαι πάλιν ἴσχυσαν.
120 οὐδὲ τὰ ἐπὶ τῶν τριάκον-
τα ἐλογίσασθε, οὐδ' ὡς
καὶ τῶν ἐπιστρατευσάν-
των καὶ τῶν ἔνδοθεν
συνεπιθεμένων αὐτῇ
125 περιεγένετο, ἀλλὰ φανε-
ροὶ ἐγένεσθε καιροφυλα-
κοῦντες τὴν πόλιν εἴ-
ποτε δοθήσεται ἐξουσί-
α λέγειν τι ἢ πράττειν κα-
130 τὰ τοῦ δήμου. εἶτα περὶ
Col. 6. καιρῶν αὐτίκα δὴ τολ-
μήσετε λέγειν τοὺς κα-

gested by Dr. Sandys, but it is doubtful whether there is room for the requisite number of letters in the lacuna.

112. ἐπείληφας: there is a blunder in the text here, and the word seems to have been finally written by a later hand. The first two letters and the last three are clear, but the middle is chaotic.

114. ἐκεῖνο: MS. εκινο.

127. τὴν πόλιν: originally written εν τηι πολει, but the preposition and the ε of πολει are cancelled by dots above them, and a ν is written in correction of the ι of τηι and as a termination to πολει. For the phrase *cf.* Demosth. *Or.* 23. § 173, p. 678.

τὰ τῆς πόλεως καιροὺς
οὐ παραφυλάξαντες, καὶ τὰ παι-
135 δία ἥκεις ἔχων εἰς τὸ δι-
καστήριον, καὶ ἀναβιβάσας
αὐτίκα δὴ ἀξιώσεις ὑπὸ
τούτων ἐλεεῖσθαι. ἀλλ' οὐ
δίκαιον· ὅτε γὰρ ἡ πό-
140 λ[ι]ς ὑπὸ τῶν ἄλλων ὠ-
κ[τ]είρετο διὰ τὰ συμβάν-
[τα], τόθ' ὑφ' ὑμῶν ἐξυβρί-
ζ[ε]το. καίτοι οὗτοι μὲν
τὴν Ἑλλάδα σώζειν προ-
145 ελόμενοι ἀνάξια τῶν
φρονημάτων ἔπασχον,
σὺ δὲ τὴν πόλιν εἰς τὰς
ἐσχάτας αἰσχύνας ἀδίκως
καθιστὰς νυνὶ δικαίως
150 τιμωρίας τεύξῃ. διὰ τί
γὰρ τούτου φείσαισθε; πό-
τερα διότι δημοτικός ἐσ-
τιν; ἀλλὰ ἴστ' αὐτὸν τοῖς μὲν
τυράννοις δουλεύειν προ-
155 ελόμενον, τῷ δὲ δήμῳ
προστάττειν ἀξιοῦντα.
ἀλλ' ὅτι χρηστός; ἀλλὰ δὶς

Col. 7. αὐτοῦ ἀ[δικί]αν κατέγνω-
τε. ναί, ἀλλὰ χρήσιμος·
160 ἀλλ' εἰ χρήσ[εσ]θε τῷ ὑφ' ὑ-

134. παραφυλάξαντες: the preposition is added above the line in another hand.
141. τὰ συμβάντα: presumably the disaster of Chaeronea. It is certain from ll. 10, 11 that this speech was delivered later than the battle of Leuctra, and Chaeronea was the only great catastrophe that befel Athens after that date. It is moreover almost the only occasion since the Persian wars on which the Athenians could represent themselves as τὴν Ἑλλάδα σώζειν προελόμενοι (ll. 145, 146).
150. τιμωρίας: MS. τειμωριας. τεύξῃ: MS. τευξη. Possibly the more Attic τεύξει should be restored.
153. ἀλλά: the second α is written above the line in correction of an ε.
158. ἀδικίαν: cf. Andoc. De Myst. § 3, p. 1, καταγνόντες αὐτῶν ἀδικίαν.

ΥΠΕΡΕΙΔΟΥ (?) ΚΑΤΑ ΦΙΛΙΠΠΙΔΟΥ.

μῶν ὁμολ[ογ]ουμένως
πονηρῷ [κρι]θέντι, ἢ 7
κρίνειν κα[κ]ῶς δόξετε
ἢ πονηρῶν [ἀν]θρώπων
165 ἐπιθυμ[εῖν. ο]ὐκοῦν οὐ-
κ ἄξιον τὰ [τούτ]ου ἀδική-
ματα αὖ[θις ἀν]αδέχεσ-
θαι, ἀλλὰ [τιμω]ρ[εῖσθαι]
τὸν ἀδικοῦντα. κ[αὶ ἐὰν]
170 ἄρα λέγῃ τις ἀναβὰς ὡς
δὶς ἥλωκεν [πρ]ότερον
παρανόμων, [κ]αὶ διὰ τοῦ-
το φῇ δεῖν ὑμᾶς ἀ[π]οψηφί-
σασθαι, τοὐναντίον ποι-
175 εἴτε κατ' ἀμφότερα. πρῶτον μὲν [γὰρ ε]ὐτύχημά
ἐστιν τὸν ὁμολογουμέ-
νως τὰ παράνομα γρά-
φοντα τὸ τρίτον κρινό-
180 μενον λαβεῖν· οὐ γὰρ
ὥσπερ ἀγαθοῦ τινὸς φεί-
δεσθαι προσήκει τού-
του, ἀλλὰ τὴν ταχίστην
ἀπηλλάχθαι, ὅς γ[ε το]ῦ
185 τρόπου δὶς ἤδη ἐν ὑμῖν
COL. 8. βάσανον δέδωκεν. ἔ-
πειτα δὲ ὥσπερ τοῖς τῶν
ψευδομαρτυριῶν δὶς ἡ-
λωκόσιν δεδώκατε ὑ-
190 μεῖς τὸ τρίτον μὴ μαρ-
τυρεῖν μηδ' οἷς ἂν παρα-
γένωνται, ἵνα μηδενὶ
τῶν πολιτῶν ᾖ τὸ ὑμέ-

163. κρίνειν : MS. κρεινειν.
173. φῇ : MS. φη.
179. κρινόμενον : MS. κρεινομενον.
193. πολιτῶν : MS. πολειτων.

ΥΠΕΡΕΙΔΟΥ (?) ΚΑΤΑ ΦΙΛΙΠΠΙΔΟΥ.

τερον πλῆθος αἴτιον
195 [τ]οῦ ἠτιμῶσθαι, ἀλλ' αὐ-
[τὸς] α[ὑ]τῷ ἀλῷ ἢ παύη-
ται τὰ ψευδῆ μαρτυρῶν,
οὕτω καὶ τοῖς ἡλωκόσι
παρανόμων ἔξεστιν
200 μηκέτι γράφειν, εἰ δὲ
μή, δῆλόν ἐστιν ὅτι ἰδί-
ου τινὸς ἕνεκα τοῦτο
ποιοῦσιν· ὥστε οὐκ οἴ-
κτου οἱ τοιοῦτοι ἄξιοί εἰ-
205 σιν ἀλλὰ τιμωρίας. ἵ-
να δὲ μὴ προθέμενος
πρὸς ἀμφορέα ὕδατος
εἰπεῖν μακρολογῶ,
ὁ μὲν γραμματεὺς ὑμῖν
210 ἀναγνώσεται τὴν γρα-
φὴν πάλιν. ὑμεῖς δὲ=
τῶν τε κατηγορημένων
COL. 9. μεμνημένοι καὶ τῶν
νόμων ἀκούσαντες
215 ἀναγιγνωσκομένων
τά τε δίκαια καὶ τὰ συμφέ-
ροντα ὑμῖν αὐτοῖς ψη-
φίζεσθε.

The following are the largest of the fragments still remaining of the earlier part of the MS.

(1) Ends of lines from the upper portion of a column. The initial letters of several lines of the succeeding column are visible on the same piece of papyrus.

195. ἠτιμῶσθαι: MS. ητειμωσθαι.
196. ἀλῷ: MS. αλω.
205. τιμωρίας: MS. τειμωριας.
207. ἀμφορέα: cf. [Dem.] Contr. Macart. p. 1052 (Or. 42, § 8).
208. εἰπεῖν is written over δεήσειεν, which has been erased.
μακρολογῶ: MS. μακρολογωι, of course a scribe's blunder who thought he was writing the dative of λόγος.
217. ὑμῖν: MS. υμειν.

ΥΠΕΡΕΙΔΟΥ (?) ΚΑΤΑ ΦΙΛΙΠΠΙΔΟΥ.

[τ]οσαντων
αις ο δ εν
εν τηι ελευ
τα των
. των η
κρατησαν
ου την
τες και
αιων τα
. ει του
χοντες
. ωχεν
νος
να ἠ·

(2) Ends of lines from the upper portion of a column.

ουκ ευχεσ
αντα τα
νατραπη
ναναι ?
σωνα παρ
και υ
σθαι εν
οις .

(3) From the top of a column.

ελευθερα πο
οις τυραννοις
ντα πραττον
εις δε υμειν

(4) Beginnings of lines.

μοκα .
λα περ
ρει φιλ
τευς α

την χ . .
τουτο δ
νηπο .
σατο εφ
μαχου .
βως γε

(5) Beginnings of lines; in some cases the first letter is lost.

. . ι τοις Ελλη
γενετο το . .
παρ ημειν κα
αλλοις πασιν
των δωρεω .
[δ]ικαιως.

(6) Beginnings of lines, from the top of a column.

εκεινο
επεμβα .
μωι εν τ
περ και
οι εισιν .
περ γαρ τ

ΔΗΜΟΣΘΕΝΟΥΣ

ΕΠΙΣΤΟΛΗ Γ.

Papyrus CXXXIII.

The roll of papyrus which contains the preceding fragment of Hyperides also holds the text of the greater part of the third of the epistles attributed to Demosthenes. A blank space of about a foot intervened (before the papyrus was divided for purposes of mounting) between the two texts, and then the Demosthenes begins, without title, but with the introductory formula Δημοσθένης τῇ βουλῇ καὶ τῷ δήμῳ χαίρειν. The length of papyrus occupied by the epistle, up to the point at which it breaks off, is 2 ft. 9 in. The text is written in twelve columns, and rather less than three more would have been required to complete the epistle. The columns are rather longer than those of the Hyperides, and contain from 29 to 36 lines, the later ones being more closely written than the earlier. In breadth they measure $2\frac{1}{4}$ in., and contain, as a rule, about 28 to 30 letters in a line; and they lean strongly to the right as in the Hyperides. The writing is in a different hand from that of the Hyperides. It is an extremely small and fine uncial, not so graceful as that of the other text, but very delicate and clear; and as it employs fewer ligatures it is in some respects easier to read at first sight, in spite of its minuteness. Palaeographically, it deserves comparison with the papyrus fragment of the Phaedo of Plato, recently discovered by Mr. Flinders Petrie, though the latter is, no doubt, considerably earlier in date. No abbreviations are used, nor do the characters occur which are found in the Hyperides to fill up a blank space at the end of a line. Pauses in the sense are marked by a circumflex stroke below the beginning of the line and a blank space in the text, and these pauses are more accurately marked than in the Hyperides. A few corrections are made in the original hand. The date of the MS. must be contemporary with that of the Hyperides, as so large a space of empty papyrus would not long be preserved unused at the end of the latter; it is therefore probably of the 2nd century B.C.

PLATE III.

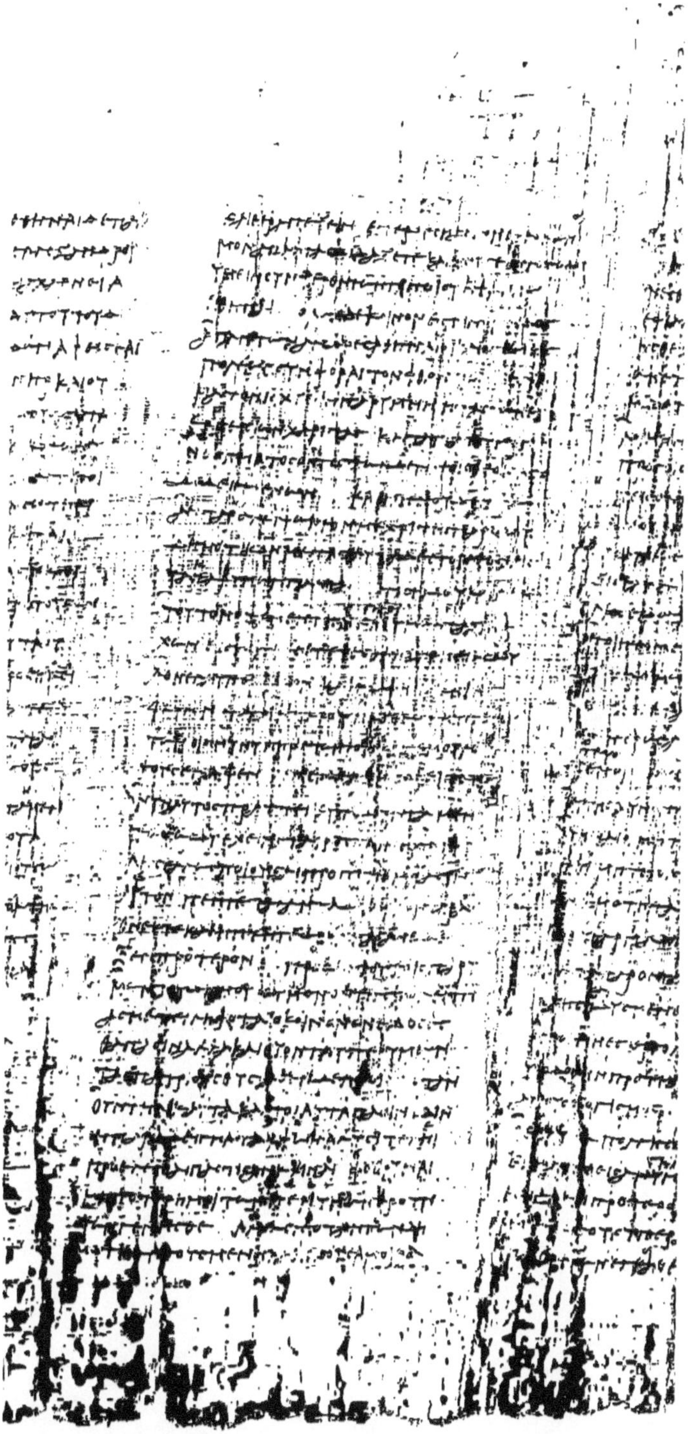

ΕΠΙΣΤΟΛΗ Γ. 57

The following collation is made with the text of Blass' revision of Dindorf (*Demosthenis Orationes*, ex recensione G. Dindorfii: editio quarta correctior, curante F. Blass, editio maior: *Bibliotheca Teubneriana*, Leipsic, 1889). References are given to the pages of Reiske, as well as to the sections in Blass' edition. There are a few classes of variations from the printed text which are not noted after their first or second occurrence. The ν ἐφελκυστικόν is often added both to nouns and verbs when no vowel follows. Final vowels are seldom elided before words beginning with a vowel. The diphthong ει is often written for the simple ι, as in κρείνω, τειμωρία, πολειτεία. The ι *adscriptum* is often added wrongly to terminations in ω or η which are not datives; *e.g.*, φανείηι, χρῆι, ἔχωι. Finally ν often stands unchanged before β, φ, &c., as in συνφέρειν, συνβαίνειν. Mis-spellings or blunders in writing are of rare occurrence. The text is incomplete, containing 38 sections out of the 45 into which Blass divides the epistle; but so far as it goes the papyrus is perfect and in good condition, except in a few places where some letters are lost through rubbing.

The letter of Demosthenes on behalf of the children of Lycurgus, even if genuine, is not of any great importance, and therefore the discovery of a new and very early evidence for its text is not of very special moment. In itself, however, the text of this MS. appears to be a good one. It contains, as all MSS. contain, a certain number of obvious scribe's blunders, but it also contains some interesting variants from the received text. Some of them seem to be improvements, such as μῆκος in § 8, ἀνθρωπινώτατα in § 12, ἂν ἔδειξεν in § 30, and the insertion of ἐάν in § 38, where it has been dropped by all the MSS. It also confirms several corrections which have been made by various scholars, and which in Blass' edition rest on their conjectures alone; thus, § 9 ὅσον for τὸ ὅσον (Blass), § 22 ἀγνῶσι for ἀγνώμοσι (Dobree), ἀδικοῖσθε for ἠδικεῖσθε or ἀδικεῖσθαι (Sauppe), § 25 οὐδείς for οὐδεὶς ἄν (Sauppe), § 27 τιν' for τήν (Blass), § 28 δ' ἐν for δέ (Reiske), § 30 πατρίους for πατρῴους (Wolf), § 31 Εὐθύδικον for Εὔδικον or Εὔδημον (Blass), § 32 γενέσθαι for γενήσεσθαι (Fuhr), besides the insertion of ἐάν in § 38, mentioned just above, which had been conjectured by Bekker. Many others are at least as good as the received text, and it is a matter of indifference whether they are accepted or not. The MSS. of Demosthenes appear to defy arrangement in families, and it is impossible to bring this one into precise relationship with those already known; but its testimony is generally on the side of S. and the other leading codices. Only in one case is there a marked divergence in phrase, when in § 13, ἐν παρρησίᾳ ζῶντες takes the place of ὄντες Ἀθηναῖοι καὶ παιδείας

ΔΗΜΟΣΘΕΝΟΥΣ

μετέχοντες, and here it is difficult to decide which version is preferable, or to explain the origin of the variation. The papyrus texts of ancient authors which have hitherto been discovered have not, as a rule, been of much textual value where the works which they contain are already known; but the present MS. seems to be of a better class than most of them, and will deserve consideration in any future critical edition of Demosthenes.

The autotype plate represents the third column from the end of the MS. (§§ 27-31 Blass, p. 1481 Reiske).

Reiske,

P. 1474. § 1. ὧν ἐμοί for ἅ μοι.
  τὴν προτέραν ἐπιστολὴν ἔγραψα for τὴν προτέραν (τὴν προτέραν ἐπιστολήν, Q) ἔπεμψα.
  ὑμεῖν for ὑμῖν: and so generally.
  συνβαίνει for συμβαίνει: and so generally.
  οὐκ ἐνποδών for ἐκποδών.
  διατρείβοντι for διατρίβοντι.
  γιγνομένοις for γεγενημένοις: so MSS.
§ 2. ἐπέστειλα μὲν οὖν for ἐπέστειλα μὲν οὖν ἄν: so Q.
  ζῶντι om.
  ποιεῖν βούλοισθε for βούλοισθε ποιεῖν.

P. 1475. § 3. δωρεάς for δωρειάς.
  αἱρούμενον for προαιρούμενον.
§ 4. βοηθήσοντας for βοηθήσαντας ἄν.
  πλήθει for δήμῳ.
  εἵλετο for εἴχετο τούτων.
  ὤετο (sic) for ἡγεῖτο.
  προσῆκεν φανερὸς ἦν for προσῆκ' ἦν φανερός.
  πάντες for ἅπαντες.
§ 5. ἐπέστειλα μὲν οὖν for ἐπέστειλα μὲν οὖν ἄν.
§ 6. ἐτειμᾶτε for ἐτιμᾶθ'.
  πώποτε for πώποθ': and so generally.
  οὕτωι for οὕτω: and so frequently with terminations in ω or η.
  κατὰ πάντα ἐνομίζετε for παρὰ πάντας ἡγεῖσθε.
  ἐκρείνατε for ἐκρίνετε.

ΕΠΙΣΤΟΛΗ Γ.

P. 1476. οὐ γὰρ ἂν ἦν (?) τοιοῦτον for οὐ γὰρ ἦν ... τοιοῦτον: so Q.
§ 7. ἐγὼ γάρ for ἐγώ· ἃ γάρ.
διεξίναι for διεξιέναι.
κρείνωι for κρίνω.
§ 8. ὑμῖν ἡγοῦμαι for ἡγοῦμαι.
ἠγνοήσατε for ἠγνοήκατε.
Λυκούργου αὐτοῦ for αὐτοῦ Λυκούργου.
μῆκος for πλῆθος.
ἀναισθησίαν for ἀναισθησίαν ἄν: so MSS.
§ 9. ἔργον om.
ὅσον for [τὸ] ὅσον.
ἄν om.
ἄλλο for τῶν ἄλλων.
ὁρᾷ (*sic*) for ὁρᾷ τις.
§ 10. ἕνεκα ταῦτα ποιεῖν for ποιεῖν εἵνεκα ταῦτα.
κἀγαθῶν om.

P. 1477. ἔδι for ἔδει.
βουλεύεσθε for βουλεύεσθαι ἐγνώκατε.
§ 11. πάντας for πάντων.
καί for ὃς καί.
ἀνουθείτητος for ἀνουθέτητος.
τε for γ': so MSS.
ὤετο for ᾤετο.
§ 12. ἀνθρωπινώτατα for ἀνθρώπινα.
ἐκινδύνευσε for διεκινδύνευσεν.
οὐ γὰρ ἦν for οὐ γάρ.
ἂν εἶναι om.
§ 13. ἐν παρρησίᾳ ζῶντες for ὄντες Ἀθηναῖοι καὶ παιδείας μετέ-χοντες.
ποεῖν for ποιεῖν. Cf. Meisterhans, *Grammatik der attischen Inschriften*, p. 44.
ὑπέρ for περί.
ὑεῖς for υἱεῖς: so elsewhere. Cf. Meisterhans, p. 47.
ποεῖν for ποιεῖν.

P. 1478. § 14. καί for ἀλλὰ καί.

ἔδει om.
§ 15. φυλάξουσι for διαφυλάξουσιν.
ὦ for ᾧ.
παρόντι for παρόντος.
§ 16. ἀποκρείναιτ' ἄν for ἀποκρίνεται.
§ 17. εἰ δὲ φήσει for εἰ δὲ μὴ φήσει.
οὐδὲ νῦν for οὐδὲ λέγειν.
προσῆκεν for προσήκει.
ἄρχειν μέν for τοὺς μὲν ἄρχειν.
ἢ ἐν οἷς for οἷς.
δεδέσθαι δέ for τοὺς δὲ δεδέσθαι.
§ 18. πολειτείᾳ for πόλει ἰσχύει.
P. 1479. τῶν τοιούτων for χαλεπὸν τοῖς τοιούτοις.
§ 19. ἧς πέρι for ἢ ἦν περί.
ποεῖσθαι for ποιεῖσθαι.
ταὐτά τε for ταῦθ'.
οἷς for ὅσοις.
οἷον om.
τοῖς Θρασυβούλου for Θρασυβούλου.
§ 20. μάλιστα συμφέρειν for συμφέρειν μάλιστα.
§ 21. ὁμοίως for ὅμως.
διασῶσαι for διασῴζειν.
§ 22. παρασχεῖν for παρέχειν.
P. 1480. § 23. ἀτυχήσωσιν for ἀτυχήσωσίν τι.
ῥᾳδίους for ῥᾳδίας.
ἑατούς for ἑαυτούς.
ἐλαττοῦσθαι ὑπάρχει for ἔλαττον ἔχειν ὑπάρξει.
τοῦτο ὅτι for ὅτι τοῦθ'.
§ 24. ἁλῶναι μὲν καταγνόντος for ἁλῶναι μὲν ὁμοίως καταγνόντος.
ὥσπερ τῶν παίδων for ὥσπερ καὶ τῶν Λυκούργου παίδων.
ποιῶν for ποιοῦντι.
§ 25. ἔφη τοὺς νόμους for τοὺς νόμους ἔφη.
καλῶν for χρηστῶν.
διὰ τούς for ἀϊδίους.
συνφέρειν for συμφέρει.

§ 26. εἰ for εἴγε.
προσήκει for συμφέρει.
οὐ μόνον τότε for οὐ μόνον.
§ 27. ἀστόν for ἑαυτόν.
P. 1481. πολιτευομένων for πολιτευόμενον.
ἄν for ἐάν.
δίκαιον for δίκαιος.
τι ποιοῦντα for ποιοῦντά τι.
§ 28. συνφοραί for συμφορά.
μᾶλλον for μεῖζον.
§ 29. Πυθέαν for τὸν Πυθέαν.
περί (corrected from καθ') ὑμῶν for ὑπὲρ ὑμῶν.
παρήει for παρῄει.
§ 30. ἐπεί for ἐπειδή.
τῶν ἄλλων om.
τως ὡς for οὕτως ὥστε.
φυλῆς for φθόης.
ἂν ἔδειξεν for ἀνέχεσθαι (ἀνέξεσθε MSS.).
§ 31. τηλικαῦτα καὶ τοιαῦτα for τοιαῦτα καὶ τηλικαῦτα.
ἰδῖν for ἰδεῖν.
ἀλυσιτελεῖ (corrected from ἀλυσιτελῇ) for ἀλυσιτελές.
τὰ τοῦ δήμου om.
P. 1182. ἄλλως τε for ἄλλως τε καί.
§ 32. ὁμοίους for ὁμοίως: so S., Q.
οἶον for οἶα.
ὅστις γνησίως εἰς ταύτην τὴν τάξιν ὑμεῖν ἑαυτόν for ὅστις εἰς ταύτην τὴν τάξιν ἑαυτὸν γνησίως ὑμῖν.
§ 33. ὕστερον πολιτευόμενοι, written as correction of εἰσελεγχόμενοι, for νῦν πολιτευόμενοι.
οὐθένα for οὐδένα.
οὔτ' ἐδεδοίκεσαν οὔτ' ἠσχύνοντο (sic) for οὔτε δεδοίκασιν οὔτε αἰσχύνονται.
ἄνδρες for ὦ ἄνδρες.
εὐνοούντων for εὔνων.
§ 34. ἣν ὑπερβολῇ for ὧν ὑπερβολῇ.

διέψευσεν for διαψεύσειεν.
εὐηθείας ἐστὶν πλήρης for ἐστὶν εὐηθείας μεστός.
μηθείς for μηδείς.

P. 1483. § 35. ταῦτα for ταῦτα δέ.
ὑμᾶς ἄν for ἄν ὑμᾶς.
ἐσμὲν οἷς for εἰμὶ ἐν οἷς.
πρώτου for πρῶτον.
§ 37. ἐπ' εὐνοίᾳ for τὴν ἐπ' εὐνοίᾳ.
γένηται for γίγνηται.
ἀφήκατε for ἀφείκατε: so S., Q.
ἐκβεβλήκατε for ἐκβεβληκότες.
§ 38. μηδὲ λαβοῦσιν for μὴ λαβοῦσι: so S. in margin.
ἔχειν *om.*

P. 1484. ἵνα ἐὰν οἷός τε ὦ, confirming Bekker's insertion of ἄν, which is omitted in the other MSS.

Ends with the two words τά τε, which immediately follow the passage just quoted.

PLATE IV.

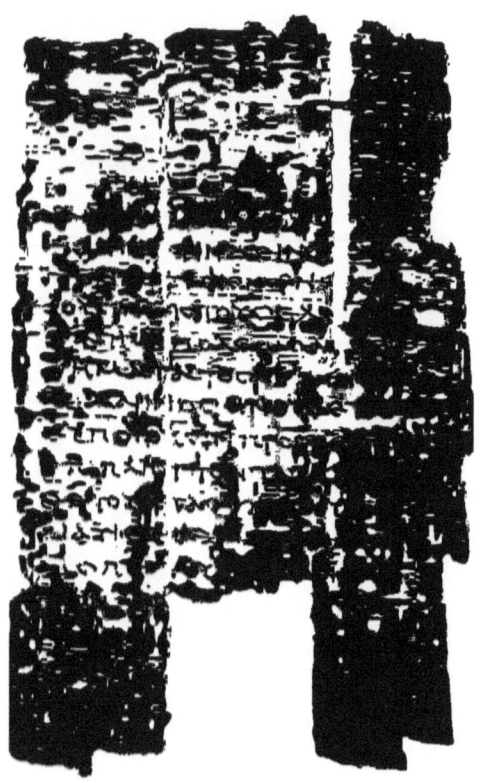

ΙΣΟΚΡΑΤΟΥΣ

ΠΕΡΙ ΕΙΡΗΝΗΣ.

Papyrus CXXXII.

THE papyrus of which a collation is here given contains the greater part of the speech (or pamphlet in the form of a speech) of Isocrates On the Peace. The last half of the papyrus, containing the text from section 62 (p. 171 d), is continuous, though not in good condition. The first half is represented by fragments alone, but there are pieces, often considerable, of every column but one from the point at which it begins, which is in the middle of the 13th section (p. 161 b). The beginning of the speech is lost. The continuous portion of the papyrus measured (before being divided in order to be mounted) 7 ft. in length, and includes 25 columns of writing, besides a blank space at the end, on which the title of the work is written. The preceding portion must have been of nearly equal length, as we have evidence of 19 columns, and the lost beginning would have occupied about four columns more. The whole roll must therefore have been nearly 14 ft. in length, and its height is 11 in. The condition of the MS. is not very good, as the papyrus is of thin texture, and the continuous portion of it is very rotten, and crumbles easily. It is also of a dark shade, and where the writing has been rubbed, as is not unfrequently the case, it is difficult to decipher. The fragments of the earlier part of the oration are in better condition, so far as they go.

The MS. is written in two hands, of which the first wrote only a comparatively small part of the text at the beginning of the speech. It is somewhat larger than the second hand, and the columns in which it is written are rather narrower. The bulk of the speech is in the second hand. The columns of this hand are 8 in. in height and $2\frac{3}{4}$ in. in breadth; and they contain on an average 45 lines, each of which, as a rule, includes about 20 to 24 letters.

The writing is uncial, of a moderate size, and regular without being ornamental. Errors in writing are not uncommon, and are often corrected in a different hand, apparently of the same date. Occasionally a note or correction has been made at the foot of a column. No abbreviations are employed, nor are there any signs to mark breaks in the sense. The general cast of the writing is moderately early, and the MS. may be ascribed to the first century of our era.

As regards the character of the text, it may be said that, in general, it resembles the papyrus MS. of the oration of Isocrates *in Nioclem* discovered some years ago, and now preserved at Marseilles (Schoene, *Melanges Graux*, 1884; Bruno Keil. *Hermes*, XIX, 596 ff.). Like it, the present MS. varies between the two chief 'families' of Isocratean MSS., now favouring one and now the other; like it, it contains a large number of independent variations, most of which are of very little value. The general drift of its testimony may be gathered from the following conspectus of passages in which (so far as its readings are legibly preserved) the papyrus agrees either with the 'vulgate' text or with the Codex Urbinas (G),—the latter being generally supported by the Ambrosianus (E).

Pap. = Vulg.

14 ὥσπερ τούς.
18 βουληθείημεν (and so with all similar forms).
20 εἰς εὐπορίαν.
36 ἐπαινέσαι.
   οὕτω ῥᾴδιον.
   πεῖσαι τοὺς ἀκούοντας.
37 ὁμοίους κελεύουσιν.
38 οὐχ ἁπάντων.
41 ποεῖσθαι τοὺς λόγους.
43 Ἑλλήνων.
46 ἀνθρώπων om.
49 ἀλλὰ γάρ.
52 τῶν κοινῶν ἁπάντων.
57 πῶς οὖν.
65 τούτων.
71 αὐτοὺς ὑμᾶς.
76 πάντας.
78 τοσοῦτο.

Pap. = G.

18 ταῦτα καλῶς.
21 ἐρήμη.
24 κατασχεῖν δυνηθείημεν.
   στρατοπέδων ξενικῶν.
29 μεγάλαι.
36 λέγωμεν.
42 τιμὴν ἐκείνοις.
50 αὐτῶν om.
52 ἐνθάδε.
   χρώμεθα συμβούλοις.
   οὐδὲν τῶν ἰδίων.
53 ὅ.
57 ἀποκριναίμην ἄν.
63 καὶ τὴν δικαιοσύνην om.
64 αἰτία τῶν κακῶν.
66 τοιαύτην.
   πᾶσι φανερὸν ποιήσειν.
68 ἐπαυσάμεθα πολεμοῦντες.
69 τυγχάνομεν.

ΠΕΡΙ ΕΙΡΗΝΗΣ.

Pap. = Vulg.

80 χρόνοις γενομένων.
82 διελόντες.
 ἐπιδεικνύντες.
83 τῶν μέν.
85 σωφρονεστέρους.
87 ἕκαστον ἐνιαυτόν.
 ἐφησθησόμενοι.
89 παράδειγμα.
 οἰκησάντων.
 μᾶλλον τῶν ἄλλων.
90 ἐν ἐνδείαις.
92 ἀποσπῶντας.
93 δεξαίμεθ' ἄν.
 πρόνοιαν ἁπάντων τούτων.
95 ἐν om.
 οἶδεν.
 σαλευθῆναι.
98 συμβαλομένων.
 ἐξέπεμψαν.
100 διῴκισαν.
 ἧτταν τήν.
102 ἐνέμενον.
106 πλείους.
115 νομίζετε πονηρῶς ἔχειν.
 ἐκεῖνοι.
119 ἰδίων.
121 οἷά περ.
126 ἀνήνεγκεν.
128 προσταγμάτων.
129 ὁρῶσι γάρ.
131 ὅτου.
133 ἐξ ὧν.
 νομίζοντες εἶναι.
136 καὶ ταῖς παρασκευαῖς.
137 ἕξουσιν.
144 αὐτοῖς αἰτίαν.

Pap. = G.

 καθεστηκυίας.
70 πολλοῖς προηγῆσθαι.
71 ἐπεχείρουν οὕτω.
 ἑτέροις.
 τοὺς ἄλλους Ἕλληνας.
72 αἰεί.
 βελτίστους.
74 διέκειτο.
 γνώσεσθε ὅσων.
76 ἐγχειρίσαι.
78 μῖσος.
80 παρόντων.
84 στρατείαν.
87 τοῦτο.
 ποιεῖν.
88 τελευτῶντες.
89 ἁπάντων τῶν ἀνθρώπων.
 δωρεαῖς om.
90 ἕξιν.
 οὐδείς om.
91 ἐπεθύμησαν.
93 παθοῦσαν.
 φροντίζει.
 μόνον (add. by corrector).
 ποιουμένων.
 μέγαν πλοῦτον.
95 οὕτως om.
 εἰ δὲ Λακεδαιμόνιοι.
96 ἐποίησαν.
 ἕξουσιν.
97 τῷ ναυτικῷ συγκινδυνευσάντων.
98 ἔφθασαν.
 τοὺς μὲν πρώτους.
99 ἐξήρκεσε.
 τυράννους.
 στάσεων καὶ πολέμων.
100 τὴν Κορινθίων.
 γεγενῆσθαι.

κ

ΙΣΟΚΡΑΤΟΥΣ

Pap. = G.

101 ἐκτῶντο γάρ.
102 τὴν κατὰ γῆν . . εὐταξίαν.
δυνάμεως.
ἐγγενομένην.
ἀπεστερήθησαν.
103 ὑπολαβόντες.
104 τοὺς . . . διεφθαρμένους.
105 τὴν ἀρχὴν ταύτην.
ἢ πῶς.
τὴν πολλὰ καὶ δεινά.
107 δεσπόται τῶν Ἑλλήνων.
111 δεινῶν ἤ.
112 τούτους om.
μηδὲν δ' ἧττον.
114 ἁπάντων αἴσχιστον κ.τ.λ.
αὐτῶν ἀγνοεῖτε.
ἐλάχιστον.
115 ἐν om. (bis).
τῶν om.
116 πεισθῆτε.
117 χώραν ἀρίστην.
ὑπαρξάντων.
οἴκους τῶν Ἑλλήνων.
118 ἀεί om.
τὴν om.
119 βελτίστους.
ἡμῶν.
120 πολύ.
τελευτήσας.
122 μόνον ἐν.
123 ἐκείνων ἐν.
φυγὰς καὶ τὰς ὑπό.
γενομένας.

Pap. = G. (continued).

124 ὡς ἐφ' ἑκατέρων.
125 τὴν μὲν πόλιν.
χεῖρον (add. by corrector).
126 χεῖρον.
127 ἡδέως ζῆν μηδέ.
128 καὶ τῶν λῃτουργιῶν κ.τ.λ.
129 τὴν ἡμέραν.
131 αὐτοί om.
βίον.
ὅπως τούς.
132 τῶν κακῶν τῶν παρόντων.
134 δεύτερον δ'.
αὐτούς om.
ἐκδίδωμεν.
135 δ' om.
τὰς δυναστείας κ.τ.λ.
136 τοὺς ἄλλους Ἕλληνας.
137 τὴν δύναμιν τὴν ἡμετέραν.
ποιήσωσιν.
138 ἀπέχεσθαι τῶν.
ἱκετείας.
139 καὶ προθύμως.
γὰρ πόλις.
140 εἰς τὴν πόλιν εἰσρυήσεσθαι.
141 δόξαν τὴν τῶν.
142 τούτων.
τῇ πόλει.
ἐξ αὐτῶν γεγενημένας.
τὰς ἐν Λακεδαίμονι βασιλείας.
144 τῆς τιμῆς ταύτης.
145 καλῶν.
τῶν ἐτῶν τῶν ἐμῶν.
καὶ λέγειν.

There are consequently 54 passages in which the papyrus supports the vulgate reading, and 123 in which it agrees with that of the Urbinas; and though it is satisfactory to find that in a large majority of instances it is in accord with the best authority for the text of Isocrates, still the considerable proportion of 'vulgate' readings which remain shows that the two families of texts had not been distinguished at the date when this copy was transcribed, especially as in many cases (see particularly §§ 93, 95) readings of both classes occur in close connection with one another. There are, moreover, eleven instances in which the corrector has altered the reading of the papyrus from one class to the other; in six of these the vulgate is corrected to the Urbinas, while in five the change is from the Urbinas to the vulgate.

Vulgate corrected to G.	G. corrected to Vulgate.
73 οὕτω corr. to οὗτος.	95 διέφθειραν corr. to διέφθειρεν.
79 συνάγοντες corr. to συναγαγόντες.	100 εἰσέβαλον corr. to ἐνέβαλον.
114 ὁμοίως corr. to τῶν ὁμοίων.	ἐπαύσαντο corr. to ἐπαύοντο.
115 μεγίστων ἀγαθῶν αἰτίαν corr. to μέγιστον τῶν ἀγαθῶν.	122 ἅ corr. to ὅ.
124 αὐτοί corr. to οὗτοι.	125 δέ struck out by corrector.
142 ἀναλογιζομένους corr. to ἀναλογισαμένους.	

The individual variations of the papyrus are numerous, but they appear to be of very little value as a rule. In many cases they concern only the order of words, and here they are often changes for the worse, introducing hiatus where it does not exist in the received text. Many more are mere obvious scribe's blunders; and only a few deserve serious consideration by future editors of the text of Isocrates. On the whole the papyrus is perhaps more valuable as evidence of the general condition of Greek classical texts about the beginning of our era than for its testimony to the actual variations in the text of the *De Pace*. It shows practically, so far as it goes, both that the texts of the classical authors preserved to us in MSS. of the tenth or later centuries are substantially the same as were in existence in the first century before or after Christ, and that variations had already found their way into those texts to a considerable extent. It tends to show that whatever corruptions exist in the texts of our classical authors had come into existence in the course of the three or four centuries following the publication of the works, when the copyists knew and spoke Greek, and are not to any great extent due to ignorant scribes and gloss-writers of later ages. Of course the evidence of two or three papyri does not go very far, but it is worth observing that the evidence of these very early MSS. does not as yet support the theory of extensive corruption of our classical texts by adscripts and glosses, while it does increase our confidence in the much later vellum MSS.

of good character; for the leading vellum MSS. of Homer and Isocrates are distinctly superior to any of the papyrus MSS. that have yet been discovered. The truth probably is that the papyrus MSS. which have so far come to light were copies made for private individuals, either by their own hands or by those of slaves, while the best vellum MSS. represent the tradition of the libraries and literary centres, where more care was bestowed alike on the text and on the transcription of it.

The following collation is made from the text of Benseler, as revised by Blass (*Isocratis Orationes,* editio altera, *Bibliotheca Teubneriana,* Leipsic, 1886); and it is from the *apparatus criticus* attached to that edition that the conspectus of the readings of the Urbinas and the vulgate has been given above. Mere errors of spelling (such as the interchange of ε and αι, ι and ει), which have generally been corrected by the reviser, have not been noticed, nor yet the omission of the ι adscript, which is common. References are given to the sections in the Benseler-Blass edition, with the pages of Stephens.

Of the two autotype plates, the first is almost the earliest fragment of the MS., containing part of the 18th section. The second, which shows the hand in which the greater part of the MS. is written, contains the conclusion of the speech.

Begins with p. 161, § 13. βουλεύησθε.

P. 161. § 13. . . ολικωτέρους for δημοτικωτέρους.
ἡμῖν for ὑμῖν.
§ 14. ἐστίν for ἐστί.
ἄλλους om.
ποιοῦσιν for ποιοῦσι.
οὕτως for οὕτω.
ὥσπερ τούς for ὥσπερ πρὸς τούς: so *vulg.*

P. 162. § 15. οὐθέν for οὐδέν.
§ 16. After εὑρήσομεν *ins.* οὔσας.
§ 18. βουληθείημεν for βουληθεῖμεν: so *vulg.*

P. 163. § 19. ἅπαντας τοὺς [τρόπους] for πάντας τρόπους (G) or πάντα τρόπον (*vulg.*).
§ 20. εἰς εὐπορίαν for πρὸς εὐπορίαν: so *vulg.*
ἐπιδώσωμεν for ἐπιδώσομεν.
§ 21. τὰς προσόδους ἢ νῦν for ἢ νῦν τὰς προσόδους.

PLATE V.

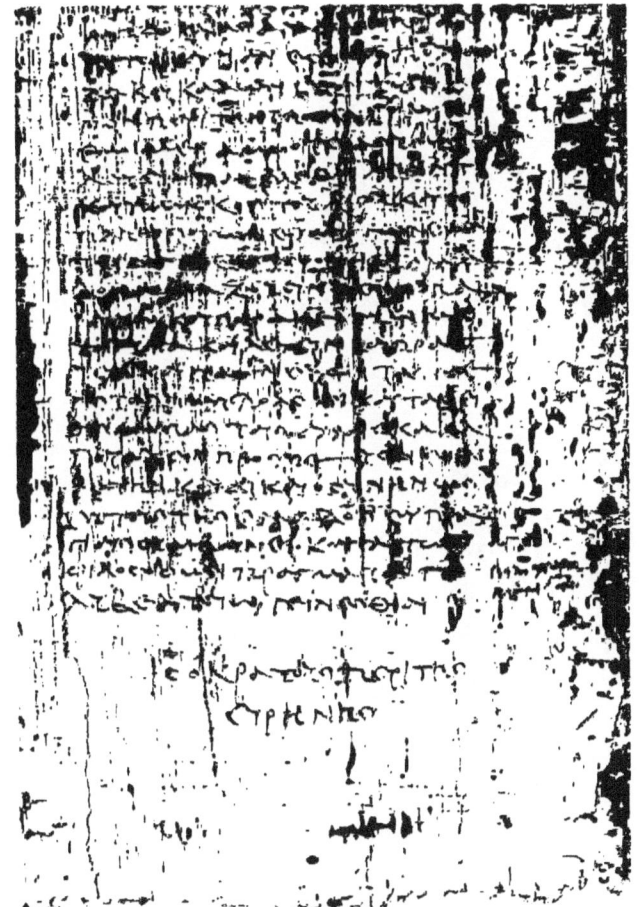

ΠΕΡΙ ΕΙΡΗΝΗΣ.

P. 164. § 24. ἂν πολλούς for πολλοὺς ἄν.
κατασχεῖν οὐκ ἂν ... θείημεν for κατασχεῖν δυνηθεῖμεν.
[ἡμεῖς τυγ]χάνομεν ἐπι[θυμοῦντε]ς for ἐπιθυμοῦντες ἡμεῖς τυγχάνομεν (G) or ἡμεῖς ἐπιθυμοῦντες τυγχάνομεν (*vulg.*).
§ 25. After τις *ins.* ἕτερα.
[μ]ή for οὐ.

P. 165. § 30. πρότερον for τὸ πρότερον.
§ 31. εἰς τοῦτο γὰρ ἀνοί[ας τινὲς ἐ]ληλύσασιν (*sic*) for εἰς τοῦτο γάρ τινες ἀνοίας ἐληλύθασιν.
τὴν ἀδικίαν for τὴν μὲν ἀδικίαν.

P. 166. § 36. ἐβουλ[όμη]ν for ἠβουλόμην.
πρόχειρον (with MSS.) for προσῆκον (Kayser's conjecture).
ἐπαινέσαι for ἐπαινεῖσθαι : so *vulg.*
οὕτω ῥᾴδιον (with Bekk.) for οὕτω πρόχειρον (Kayser and Blass), οὕτω προσῆκον (GE), or οὕτω καὶ ῥᾴδιον (*vulg.*).
ἡμῖν [ἐθέλοντας] for ἐθέλοντας ἡμῖν.
§ 37. ὁμοίους κε[λεύουσιν] for κελεύουσιν ὁμοίους : so *vulg.*
πότερα for πότερον.
[συμβουλεύο]υσι ὑμῖν for συμβουλεύουσιν ὑμῖν.
ὑμᾶς for ἡμᾶς.

P. 167. § 38. οὐχ ἁπάντων for οὐ πάντων : so *vulg.*
§ 40. καταγέλαστόν τ[ι] for καταγέλαστον.
§ 41. ποεῖσθαι τοὺς λόγους for τοὺς λόγους ποιεῖσθαι : so *vulg.*
ἐλθών for ἐπελθών.
ἔχομεν (so MSS.) for ἀξιοῦμεν (quotation in Dion. Hal.).

P. 168. § 43. Ἑλλήνων (so *vulg.*) for ἄλλων (G).
ἐτόλ[μησαν] ἐ[κλι]πεῖν for ἐκλιπεῖν ἐτόλμησαν.
§ 44. δεῖ for δεῖν.
§ 46. In the line above καὶ δασμ[ολογοῦμεν] are the characters των ιδια (for [αὐ]τῶν λυμαινόμεθα).
ἀνθρώπων *om.* : so *vulg.*
§ 47. οὐ μόνον repeated by inadvertence.

P. 169. § 48. τριήρεις εἰ πληροῖεν for εἰ τριήρεις πληροῖεν.

ΙΣΟΚΡΑΤΟΥΣ

τὴν πολεμίων for τὴν τῶν πολεμίων.
ἐγβαίνουσιν for ἐκβαίνουσιν.

§ 50. The line between ἐπικε[ιμένης] and τοὺς τοῦτο, where the received text has ἦν τις ἁλῷ δεκάζων, contains the characters ραν τούτους α . . .
τῶν πολιτῶν διαφθεῖραι for διαφθεῖραι τῶν πολιτῶν.

§ 52. [λόγων] τε for λόγων.
The passage πραγμάτων ὄντες οὕτως ἀλογίστως ἔχομεν ὥστε περὶ κ.τ.λ. has been confused somehow, the letters visible being πραγματ . . . . . . ον [*corr.* ου] . . . ως εχομε . . . . . . περι κ.τ.λ.

P. 170. τῶν κοινῶν ἁπάντων for ἁπάντων τῶν κοινῶν : so *vulg*.
οὐθείς for οὐδείς.

§ 53. ἂν ὁμολογήσαιμεν for ὁμολογήσαιμεν ἄν.
ὡς is inserted above the line before πιστοτάτους.
εἶναι *om*.

§ 56. γενομένας for ἐγγεγενημένας (G) or γεγενημένας (*vulg*.).
ἐπιχε[ιρ]ῆσαι[μεν] for ἐπιχειροίην.

§ 57. τάχα δ' ἄν τις for τάχ' ἂν οὖν τις.
πῶς οὖν for πῶς : so *vulg*.
τυγχάνομεν κεκτημένοι for κεκτημένοι τυγχάνομεν.

P. 171. § 63. εὐδοκιμή[σειν] for εὐδαιμονήσειν.
καὶ τὴν δικαιοσύνην *om*. : so GE.

P. 172. παιδευθείημεν for παιδευθεῖμεν : so *vulg*.

§ 65. χαλεπώτατον first hand, corrected to χαλεπόν.
τούτων (*vulg*.) for τοῦτον (G).

P. 173. § 68. At foot of column, as note on πρὶν ἠθέλησαν Λακεδαιμόνιοι ποιήσασθαι τὰς συνθήκας is the reading πρὶν [ἠ]ναγκάσαμεν Λακεδαιμ[ονίου]ς ποιήσασθ'.

§ 69. πολιτίας for πολιτείας.
δυνηθείημεν for δυνηθεῖμεν (*bis*) : so *vulg*.

§ 70. δέξασθαι τῇ πόλει διδομένην for δέξασθαι διδομένην τῇ πόλει (G) or διδομένην δέξασθαι τῇ πόλει (*vulg*.).

§ 71. αὐτοὺς ὑμᾶς for αὐτούς : so *vulg*.
τοιούτων for τῶν τοιούτων.

ΠΕΡΙ ΕΙΡΗΝΗΣ.

§ 72. ἀλλήλοις first hand (with E and Blass) corrected to ἀλλήλαις (G *vulg*.).
αἰεί for ἀεί.
γνώμην ἔχειν ὑμᾶς for ὑμᾶς γνώμην ἔχειν.

§ 73. τὰς πονηρίας first hand (with GE), corrected to τὰς πονηράς (Bekk.), for τάς τε πονηρίας (*vulg*. τάς τε πονηράς).
γινομένας for γιγνομένας, and so throughout.
οὕτω first hand (and so *vulg*.), corrected to οὗτος (G).

P. 174. § 75. ἦν om.
Ὑπερβούλου for Ὑπερβόλου. A column ends with the syllables Ὑπερ, and before the termination -βουλου at the beginning of the next another hand has added the letters Ευ, evidently taking υπερ as a preposition and desiring to complete the proper name.
οὐδὲ κενῶν ἐλπίδων for οὐδ' ἐλπίδων κενῶν.

§ 76. πάντας for ἅπαντας : so *vulg*.
εἰσβάλλοντας is corrected in another hand from ἐμβάλλοντας.
ἐν τοῖς ... κινδύνοις is corrected to τῶν ... κινδύνων.
τῶν πόλεων αὐτῷ for αὐτῷ τῶν πόλεων.

§ 77. εὐδοκούσης for εὐδοκιμούσης.
οὐθείς for οὐδείς.
ἐπιστρατεύ[σ]αντας for ἐπιστρατεύοντας.

§ 78. τοσοῦτο for τοσοῦτον : so *vulg*.
κατέστησαν first hand (and so G), corrected to κατέστησεν.

§ 79. ἄρχοντες for ὑπάρχοντες.
πολλὰ δεινά for πολλὰ καὶ δεινά.
ἔσχον γνώμην for γνώμην ἔσχον.
ἡμᾶς is corrected to ἡμῶν.
συνάγοντες first hand (and so *vulg*.), corrected to συναγαγόντες (G).

P. 175. τὰ ἐκείνων for τἀκείνων.

§ 80. χρόνοις γενομένων for πράγμασιν ἐγγενομένων (πράγμασιν γιγνομένων GE): so *vulg*.

ἂν ἴσως for ἴσως ἄν.

§ 81. φαῦλον first hand, but corrected to φλαῦρον.
λυπησάντα first hand (so Cobet, Blass), corrected to λυπήσοντα (so *vulg.*).

§ 82. ἐξεύρισκον first hand for εὕρισκον, but the ἐξ is cancelled.
ἂν ἄνθρωποι τὰ μάλιστα for ἄνθρωποι μάλιστ' ἄν.
τῶν φόρων for τῶν πόρων (GE) or ἐκ τῶν φόρων (*vulg.*).
ἐπιδεικνύντες for ἐπιδεικνύοντες : so *vulg.*
ἄλλοις συμμάχοις for συμμάχοις.
Ἕλλησιν for Ἕλλησι.

§ 83. αὐτὴν τήν for αὐτοί τε τήν.
ζηλοῦντες καὶ θαυμάζοντες for θαυμάζοντες καὶ ζηλοῦντες.
ἤμελλεν for ἤμελλε.

§ 84. ἐμβεβληκότων for εἰσβεβληκότων: so MSS.
Δεκελιᾶσι συνεστηκότος for Δεκελειᾶσιν ἑστηκότος or Δεκελεικοῦ συνεστηκότος (*vulg.*). Δεκελιᾶσι has accent by first hand.
στρατείαν for στρατιάν (G) or στρατιάς (*vulg.*).

P. 176. τοῦτο ἀφροσύνης for τοῦτ' ἀφροσύνης.

§ 85. ποιοῦσι σωφρονεστέρους for ποιοῦσιν ἐμφρονεστέρους : so *vulg.*

§ 86. κακοῖς καὶ μείζοσι for καὶ μείζοσι (GE) or καὶ μείζοσι κακοῖς (*vulg.*).
πληρώμασιν for τοῖς πληρώμασι.
δὲ τῷ Δεκελικῷ πολέμῳ for Δάτῳ δέ (GE) or δὲ τῷ Πόντῳ (*vulg.*). The letters Δε are added above the line, and there has been some confusion in writing the word.
τεσσεράκοντα for τετταράκοντα.

§ 87. κατὰ πέντε for πέντε.
ταφὰς ποιεῖν τῶν ἐνκυκλίων for τῶν ἐγκυκλίων ταφὰς ποιεῖν, but a stroke above each of these four words probably indicates that the order should be changed.
ἕκαστον ἐνιαυτόν for ἕκαστον τὸν ἐνιαυτόν: so *vulg.*
καί *om.* before τῶν ἀστυγειτόνων.

ΠΕΡΙ ΕΙΡΗΝΗΣ.

ἀλλ' ἐφησθησόμενοι for ἀλλὰ συνηδόμενοι (from Pollux) or ἀλλὰ συνησθησόμενοι (GE): so *vulg.*

§ 88. ἐπεθυμοῦμεν for ἐπιθυμοῦμεν.

§ 89. παράδειγμα for δεῖγμα: so *vulg.*
φανείημεν for φανεῖμεν: so *vulg.*
εὐδαιμονίζειν is corrected to εὐδαίμονα νομίζειν.
οἰκησάντων for οἰκισάντων: so *vulg.*

P. 177. στέργοντας δ' is corrected to καὶ χαίροντας.

§ 90. ἔχοντες for σχόντες.
λέγω δὲ ταῖς τῆς πόλεως δικαιοσύναις first hand for ἐπὶ δὲ τῇ τῆς πολιτείας δικαιοσύνῃ, but corrected in another hand.

§ 91. ἐστίν for ἐστί.
καθέστηκεν for καθέστηκε.
ἑαυτοῖς for αὐτοῖς.

§ 92. ἀντὶ γάρ for ἀντὶ μὲν γάρ.
φρουρεῖν is corrected from φρονεῖν.
ἀποσπῶντας for ἀποσπῶντες: so *vulg.*

§ 93. ἐστίν for ἐστί.
μήτε παίδων is added in another hand above the line.
μόνον is added in another hand above the line.

P. 178. πρόνοιαν ἁπάντων τούτων for πρόνοιαν (GE) or πρόνοιαν ἁπάντων τῶν τοιούτων (*vulg.*).
μηθέν for μηδέν.
ἔχειν is added in another hand above the line before βίον.

§ 94. ἐστίν for ἐστί.

§ 95. χώραν first hand for πόλιν, but corrected in another hand.
ἐκείνοις for ἐν ἐκείνοις.
ἐπεδείξαντο ... αὐτῶν first hand for ἐπεδείξατο ... αὐτῆς, but corrected.
πεντακοσίοις first hand for ἑπτακοσίοις, but corrected.
οὐθείς for οὐδείς.
σαλευθῆναι for σαλεῦσαι: so *vulg.*
ἐποίησαν first hand for ἐποίησεν, but corrected.

§ 96. ἐνέπλησαν first hand for ἐνέπλησεν, but corrected.

ὑπερέβαλον for ὑπερεβάλοντο.
ὑπάρχουσιν for ὑπάρχουσι.

P. 179. § 98. ἐπεβούλευσαν is corrected to ἐπεβούλευον.
στρατιάν is corrected from στρατείαν.
ἐξέπεμψαν for ἀνέπεμψαν : so *vulg*.
καί is prefixed to Χίων above the line in another hand.

§ 99. ἐξαμαρτάνειν first hand for ἐξαμαρτεῖν, but corrected.
ταῦτα for ταῦτ'.

§ 100. ἀφείλαντο for ἀφείλοντο.
εἰσέβαλον (G) is corrected to ἐνέβαλον (*vulg*.).
ἐπαύσαντο (G) is corrected to ἐπαύοντο (*vulg*.).
φασίν for φασί.

§ 101. ἐπὶ τελευτῆς γενομένοις for ἐπιγιγνομένοις or ἐπὶ τῇ τελευτῇ γιγνομένοις (*vulg*.).
ταύτην is added above the line in another hand.
γενέσθαι for γεγενῆσθαι.
Accent on ἐκτῶντο, qu. first hand?

§ 102. A mark in the margin opposite μελετωμένην refers to a note at the foot of the page, of which only the last two words are visible, μελετῶν ῥᾳδι^ω.

P. 180. ἀκολασίαν is corrected to ἀπορίαν.
ταύτης *om*.

§ 103. αὐτοῖς is added above the line in another hand.

§ 104. πράξεσιν for πράξεσι.
ἁμαρτήμασιν for ἁμαρτήμασι.

§ 105. φυγεῖν for φεύγειν.
ἐπαίρασαν (corrected from ἐπέροσαν) for ἐπάρασαν.

§ 106. εἰ δὲ τόν for εἰ τόν, but the δέ is perhaps meant to be cancelled.
ἐφ' for ὑφ'.

P. 181. § 107. οὕτως for οὕτω.
ἐκεῖνοι . . . τῶν πραγμάτων *om*., but ἐκεῖνοι . . προέστησαν (*sic*) added at foot of column.
After ἐπιπολάσαι καί there is a semicircular mark referring to the foot of the column, where ἐπὶ πολλὰς ἀρχὰς προελθεῖν καί is added.

ΠΕΡΙ ΕΙΡΗΝΗΣ.

§ 110. αἰεί for ἀεί.
μᾶλλον is added above the line.
Opposite ἀγνοοῦσι the word ἀστοχοῦσι is written in the margin.
μηθείς for μηδείς.
αὐτούς for αὐτοῖς.

§ 111. ἔχοντας for ὄντας.
ἢ χαλεπῶν for ἢ τῶν χαλεπῶν.

§ 112. [κακ]ὸν οὐδέν for οὐδὲν κακόν.

P. 182. οὕς is corrected to οἷς.
οὐδέποτε for οὐδεπώποτ'.
μηδὲν δέ: the δέ has been struck out.

§ 113. For ἔτι δέ, ὅλον δέ in margin.
ὅπου δὲ οἱ is written in the margin; there appears to have been some confusion in the text, but the papyrus is mutilated here.
ἀρχάς is written in the margin, apparently as correction of δόξας.
τί and τοὺς ἄλλους are added above the line, the former before θαυμάζειν.
τοιούτων is added above the line.
ἐπιθυμοῦσι for ἐπιθυμοῦσιν.

§ 114. ἀπεδέξασθε (corrected from ἀποδέχεσθαι) for ἀποδέχεσθε.
τι πάντων for πάντων.
ταῦτ' is added above the line.
ὁμοίως (as vulg.) corrected to τῶν ὁμοίων (as G and Bekk.).

§ 115. ὑπολαμβάνετε for ἡγεῖσθε.
μεγίστων ἀγαθῶν αἰτίαν first hand (so vulg.), corrected to μέγιστον τῶν ἀγαθῶν (GE).
πράξεσιν for πράξεσι.
ἐπεί for ὅτι.
ἐκεῖνοι for κεῖνοι: so vulg.
πάντα δέοντα first hand for πάντα τὰ δέοντα, and a corrector has struck out παν.

ΙΣΟΚΡΑΤΟΥΣ

§ 116. φιλοσοφήσατε καὶ σκέψασθε first hand for φιλοσοφήσετε καὶ σκέψεσθε, but corrected.
τὼ πόλ[ε]ε τούτω (corrected from τῇ πόλ[η?] ταῦτα) for τὼ πόλη τούτω.
τήν before Λακεδαιμονίων, *om.*; after Λακεδαιμονίων ins. ἀρχήν.

P. 183. § 117. οὐδὲ ἀργυρεῖα for οὐδ' ἀργυρεῖα.

§ 118. ἄλλοι τινὲς τὰς ἀκροπόλεις for τὰς ἀκροπόλεις ἄλλοι τινές; and μέν and ἀεί are added in another hand.
πλέον ἢ δισχιλίων corrected to πλεόνων τρισχιλίων.
βούλωνται first hand for βούλονται, but corrected.
διοικοῦσι for διοικοῦσιν.
ὑμετέρας first hand for ἡμετέρας, but corrected.

§ 119. γιγνομένην is corrected from γενομένην.
ἰδίων for ἰδιωτῶν: so *vulg.*
ἀσφαλεστάτους first hand for ἀσφαλέστατα ζῆν, but corrected.
οἴσθε for οἴεσθε.
τοιοῦτο for τοιοῦτον.

§ 120. καὶ .... ἀνθρώπων overlined as if to be cancelled. A mutilated marginal note appears to refer to this, but only the letters αρ .... φευγ ... remain.

§ 121. δῆμον is corrected from a mutilated reading which begins πολεδ ....
λυμενομένους for λυμαινομένους. ε often is substituted for αι in this MS. and *vice versa*, but usually they are corrected.

§ 122. ἅ (G) first hand for ὅ (*vulg.*), but corrected.

P. 184. ἔχοντες for ἔχοντας.
ὅμοια corrected to ὁμοίως.
καίτοι γε first hand for καὶ ταῦτ' εἰδότες, but corrected in margin.

§ 123. δομοκρατίαν for δημοκρατίαν.
ἐπεὶ μέν for ἐπὶ μέν.
ἐν is added above the line in another hand.

ΠΕΡΙ ΕΙΡΗΝΗΣ.

§ 124. ἐφ' ἑκατέρων is corrected to ἐφ' ἑκάτερον, and in the margin ἐπ' ἀμφότερα appears to be written.
τῆς .. πονηρίας first hand for ταῖς .. πονηρίαις, but corrected.
ὥσθ' ... ταραχάς, *om.* in text, added at head of column.
αὐτοί first hand (and so *vulg.*), corrected to οὗτοι (G).
τούτους δέ corrected to τοὺς δέ.

§ 125. ὀλιγαρχίας for ὀλιγαρχίαις.
τούτους δὲ διά corrected to τούτους διά, as *vulg.*
εὐδαιμονοστάτους (*sic*) for εὐδαίμονας (*vulg.*) or εὐδαιμονεστέρους (G).

§ 126. καὶ παραλαβών for παραλαβών.
τὸν αὑτοῦ ἐλάττω for ἐλάττω τὸν αὑτοῦ.

§ 127. τολμῶσι for τολμῶσιν.

P. 185. § 128. πρὸ σφᾶς for πρὸς σφᾶς.
λητουργιῶν (*sic*) for λειτουργιῶν.
τοσαύτας for τοιαύτας.
πενουμένους for πενομένους.

§ 129. ἐστίν for ἐστί.
ἡμέραν ἑκάστην is corrected to ἡμετέραν ἀγοράν, but the original reading is restored in a note at the foot of the column.
μᾶλλον for μάλιστα.
ὁρῶσι γάρ for ὁρῶντες : so *vulg.*
τὰ βέλτιστα λέγοντας first hand for τῶν τὰ βέλτιστα λεγόντων, but corrected.

§ 130. αὑτοῖς is corrected to αὑτούς.

§ 131. μὲν ταύταις for ἐν ταύταις.
ὄντας, *om.*
σκοποῦσι for σκοποῦσιν.
ὅτου for οὗ : so *vulg.*
ἐκπορίζουσι (corr. from πορουσι) for ἐκποριοῦσιν.
ἀλ' for ἀλλ', and so elsewhere.
δοκοῦντας ἔχειν for ἔχειν τι δοκοῦντας.
ἀπορουμένοις is written in margin as correction of ἀπόροις.

§ 132. διείλεγμαι μὲν γάρ for διείλεγμαι μέν, the γάρ being added above the line.
ἐπ' αὐτά for αὐτά.
§ 133. ἐστίν for ἐστί.
ἂν after ἐξ ὧν, om.: so vulg.
βουληθείημεν for βουληθεῖμεν: so vulg.
νομίζοντες εἶναι for εἶναι νομίζοντες: so vulg.

P. 186. καλοὺς καὶ ἀγαθούς for καλούς τε καγαθούς.
γείνοντες for γνόντες.
οὐθεὶς οὐθέτερον for οὐδεὶς οὐδέτερον: in the margin is written οὐδὲν ἕτερον.
§ 134. αὐτονόμους is added above the line in another hand.
§ 135. τρίτον ἐάν for τρίτον δ' ἦν.
ποιῆσθε for ἡγῆσθε.
μετὰ . . θεούς om., but added at foot of column.
ἑκάστῳ first hand for ἑκόντες, but corrected.
§ 136. ἦν μὲν οὖν for ἦν οὖν, the μέν being an addition above the line in another hand.
τῶν for τῷ.
τοὺς ἄλλους Ἕλληνας for τοὺς Ἕλληνας: so G.
§ 137. τολμήσει οὐδεμία for οὐδεμία τολμήσει.
ἕξουσιν for ἄξουσιν: so vulg.
§ 138. προηκούσαις is written in the margin opposite προεχούσαις.
ἦν τέ πως for ἦν τε.
κ[αὶ] πολλάς for πολλάς.

P. 187. § 139. καὶ δυναμένους om., but added at foot of column, and the καί before βουλομένους is added above the line in a later hand.
§ 140. τοιαύτης ἡμῖν εὐνοίας for τοιαύτης εὐνοίας ἡμῖν.
ὑπαρξάσης is corrected to ὑπαρχούσης.
τίνας δ' οὐκ ἐπαινέσεσθαι is added at head of column; lacuna in text at this passage.
§ 141. τῶν Ἑλλήνων is corrected to τῶν ἄλλων Ἑλλήνων.
σωτηρίας for σωτῆρας. At the foot of the column is a different reading of the whole clause, perhaps

ΠΕΡΙ ΕΙΡΗΝΗΣ. 79

     suggested by the difficulty caused by this corruption
     of σωτῆρας into σωτηρίας, —σαντας περὶ τῆς τῶν ἄλλων
     Ἑλλήνων ἐλευθερίας καὶ σωτηρίας γ[ε]νηθῆναι.
§ 142. ἐκεῖνο for ἐκεῖν'.
    δοκιμάζειν is apparently corrected to συνδοκιμάζειν.
    ἀπολύσασθαι first hand for διαλύσασθαι, but corrected.
    τάς before δυναστείας is apparently meant to be cancelled
     by a line drawn above it.
    ἀναλογιζομένους (*vulg.*) first hand for ἀναλογισαμένους
     (G), but corrected.
§ 143. μακαριστότατοι for μακαριστότεροι.
    τυραννίδας καὶ τὰς πόλεις ἐχόντων, for τυραννίδας κατεχόντων: κατεχόντων in marg. apparently as correction
     for καὶ . . ἐχόντων.
    ὅσῳ for ὅσον.
    λιπόντων . . ἀποβαλόντων for λειπόντων . . ἀποβαλλόντων.
§ 144. ἔνεστιν δὲ καί for ἔνεστι δ' ἐν.
    ὑπολάβωσιν for ὑπολάβωσι.
    ὑμετέραν for ἡμετέραν.
P. 188. αὐτοῖς αἰτίαν for αἰτίαν αὐτοῖς : so *vulg.*
§ 145. ἐνόντων λόγων for λόγων ἐνόντων.
    ἢ ἐγώ for ἠγώ.
    καὶ πράττειν *ins.* after λέγειν.
    φιλοσόφων : πολιτευομένων in marg.

At the foot of the last column is the title
    Ἰσοκράτους περὶ τῆς
     εἰρήνης
and again in the middle of the blank space following the last column,
    Ἰσοκράτους
    περὶ εἰρήνης.

ΟΜΗΡΟΥ ΙΛΙΑΔΟΣ

Α

Papyrus CXXIX.

This papyrus contains three small and unimportant fragments of the first book of the Iliad, which would not be worth including in this volume except for the sake of completeness. The largest of them only measures 6 in. in height and 4¼ in. in breadth; and of this the lower part is frayed out so as to destroy the writing, and half the breadth is occupied by blank margin. The hand is a small and comparatively late one, and the ink is very black. The writing is on the *verso* of the papyrus, and on the *recto* there are remains of something of the nature of accounts. The portions of the text of the Iliad contained on these fragments are (1) the ends of ll. 37–54, (2) a few letters of ll. 65–67, (3) the ends of ll. 207–229. The variants are of no importance, and, such as they are, they indicate that the MS. was not of high character. They are:—

Il. I. 209 κηδομένη ται for κηδομένη τε.
213 παρέστασε for παρέσσεται.
214 ἡμεῖν for ἡμῖν.
217 ἄμινον for ἄμεινον.

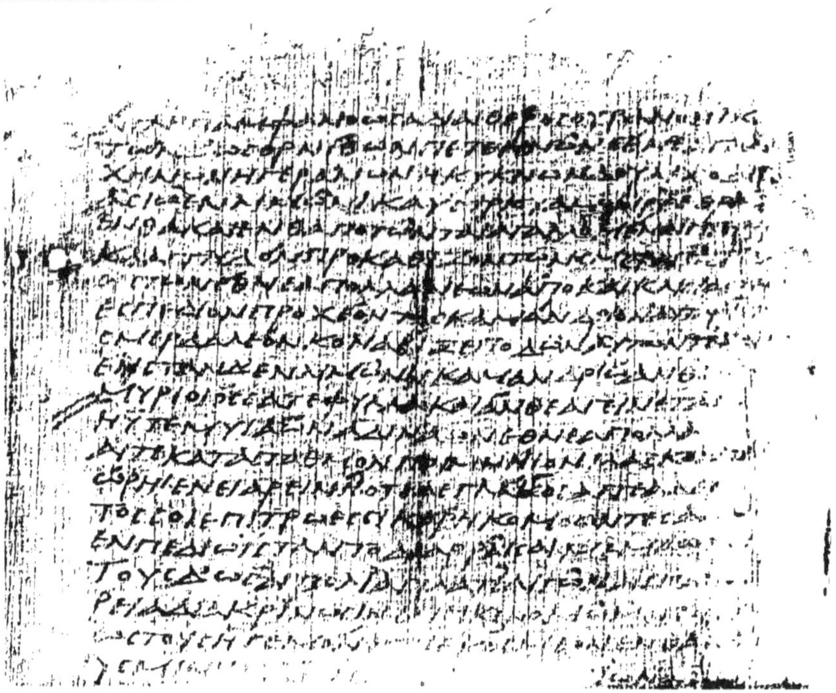

ΟΜΗΡΟΥ ΙΛΙΑΔΟΣ

Β Γ Δ

Papyrus CXXVI recto.

This MS., which is the longest papyrus manuscript of Homer that has yet come to light, was obtained by Mr. A. C. Harris from the 'Crocodile Pit' at Ma'abdeh, in which he had previously discovered the MS. of the eighteenth book of the Iliad (Papyrus CVII), the text of which has been published in the *Catalogue of Ancient Manuscripts in the British Museum*, part I. The discovery of the present MS. was made in 1854, but the papyrus did not come into the possession of the Museum until 1888. It begins with l. 101 of the second book of the Iliad, and proceeds continuously as far as l. 40 of the fourth book. It is noticeable, however, that the Catalogue in book II. (ll. 494–877) is omitted, though the lines of invocation (484–493) which precede it are included. A marked peculiarity of this papyrus is its arrangement in the form of a book, not in that of a roll. It consists (in its present condition) of nine sheets, each of which is folded so as to form two leaves; and holes remain through which strings were passed in order to bind the sheets together. All nine sheets belong to a single quire. The text is written on one side only of each leaf, the other side being originally left blank, though three of these blank pages have been subsequently used to contain the text of the grammatical treatise entitled Τρύφωνος τέχνη γραμματική, which is printed on pp. 111–116 of the present volume, and a fourth contains some half-obliterated accounts. The Homer occupies, therefore, eighteen columns or pages, each of which contains on an average 48 to 50 lines. The height of the papyrus is 11¾ inches. The condition of the papyrus is very fair, except that the last few letters of nearly every line are lost, and the whole is stained a deep brown colour, which makes the writing in many places very difficult to read.

82   ΟΜΗΡΟΥ

The MS. is of comparatively late date, probably not earlier than the 4th or 5th century, and the text is far from being a good one. As originally written it was full of blunders of orthography or of transcription, but many of these have been corrected, some perhaps by the original hand, some certainly by a different one. Certain faults of orthography are chronic, such as the spelling of the names Ὀδυσσεύς and Ἀχιλλεύς with double σσ or double λλ even when the metre requires the single letter, the substitution of αι for ε, and occasionally οι for υ, and the interchange of ει and ι. Accents, breathings, and marks of elision are written throughout, usually in the first hand, though not a few words remain unaccented and the accentuation does not always follow the received rules. In a few instances a dot is used to indicate pauses or to separate words, after the manner described by Prof. B. Keil in his account of the Marseilles papyrus of Isocrates (*Hermes*, XIX. 612); *e.g.* III. 333 Λυκάονος· ἥρμοσε, 379 ἄψ· ἐπόρουσε, 387 εἰροκόμῳ· ἥ. Two oblique lines in the margin are generally used to denote the beginning of a speech or some other break in the narrative. The hand is a somewhat coarse sloping uncial, with the exception of the last column, which is in a lighter and more irregular hand of the same period. The number of lines in each column is stated at the foot of it, though in some cases the figure has been lost.

The collation of this and all the following Homeric texts has been made with Mr. W. Leaf's edition of the Iliad (London, 1886 and 1888).

The autotype plate represents the top of the eighth column of the MS. and includes the text of book II. ll. 458–477.

Il. II.   103 διακτόρῳ is corrected from διακτόρι. ἀργιφόντῃ for ἀργειφόντῃ, and similarly *passim*.
105 Ἀτρέω for Ἀτρέι.
108 νήσοισι is corrected from νηυσί.
109 ἔπε' is corrected from ἐπ'.
111 με is corrected from μέν.
112 μέν is omitted.
115 πάντ', apparently, for πολύν.
117 πολάων for πολλάων. κατέλυσα for κατέλυσε.
120 τε is omitted.
123 καὶ θέλοιμεν for κ' ἐθέλοιμεν.
124 ἀριθμηθήμενε (corrected from ἀριθμηθέμενε) for ἀριθμηθήμεναι.

ΙΛΙΑΔΟΣ Β.   83

The rest of this column is undecipherable, with the exception of a few words in each line, owing to the deep brown colour to which the papyrus has been stained.

152 ἄπταισθαι for ἄπτεσθαι.
153 δ' for τ'. αὐτήν for αὐτὴ δ'. οὐρανόν is corrected from οὐρόν.
155 ὑπέρμορα is corrected from ὑπέρμενα.
156 Ἀθηναίην is corrected from Ἀθηναίη.
158 δή is corrected from δέ.
160 δ' ἔχεν for δέ κεν.
161 εἵνεκα is corrected from ἕνεκα.
163 μετά for κατά. χαλκοχειτώνων (sic) is written over erasure of μηδέ τ' ἐρώει (l. 179).
164 σοῖς δ' for σοῖς.
166 ἔφαθ' for ἔφατ'.
168 is omitted.
170 μελαίνης is corrected to μελένης.
176 δ' ἔχεν for δέ κεν. Πριάμῳ is corrected from Πριάμου.
179 μετά for κατά. μηδέ τ' ἐρώει is written over erasure of χαλκοχιτώνων (l. 163).
181 μηδ' ἔα (corrected from μηδέ) for μηδὲ ἔα.
184 Ἰθακήσειος (corrected from Ἰθακήσεις) for Ἰθακήσιος.
189 ἀγενοῖς for ἀγανοῖς.
192 Ἀτρείδαο for Ἀτρείωνος.
193 υἷες for υἷας.
196 θυμὸς δὲ μέγας is written over erasure of ἐν βουλῇ δ' ἐν πα . . . .
198 βοόωντα is corrected from βοῶντα.
202 οὐδέ . . οὐδ' for οὔτε . . οὔτ'.
205 ἔδωκεν for δῶκε.
206 is omitted.
208 αὖθις for αὖτις. κε for καί.
210 βρέμετε for βρέμεται.
212 Θαρσίτης for Θερσίτης. ἐκολῴα is corrected from κολῴ[α].
213 ὄσσ' for ὅς ῥ'.
214 ἐριζέμεναι is corrected from ἀριζέμενε.

217 φολκὸς δ' for φολκός.
218 συνοχωκέτες for συνοχωκότε.
219 Ἀχιλλῆι.. Ὀδυσσῆι for Ἀχιλῆι.. Ὀδυσῆι, and so *passim*.
221 τούς for τώ.
225 δ' for δή. χατίζεις is corrected from κα[τίζεις].
229 οἴσει is corrected from ὔσει.
233 τ' is corrected from δ'.
249 Ἀτρείδης is corrected from Ἀτρείδη.
251 δέ for the second τε.
257 τό is corrected from σύ.
258 ἀφραίνοντα, κιχήσομαι, νύ περ, are corrected from ἀφρένοντα, κιχήσομεν, ὑπέρ.
262 The second τ' is corrected from δ'.
266 ἰδνώθη is corrected from ἰγνώθη, and θαλερόν from δαλερόν.
267 μεταφρένου is corrected from μετάφρενον.
269 ἀπομόρξατο δάκρυ is corrected from ἐς πλησίον ἄλλον (l. 271).
270, 271 are omitted, but are added at top of column.
273 βουλάς is corrected from βουλά.
275 λωβητῆρα is corrected from λωβητάς.
276 θήν, αὖτις, are corrected from θή, αὖθις.
277 νεικείειν is corrected from νεικείην.
278 πτολίπορθος is corrected from πτολίεθρος.
286 ἤπερ for ἤνπερ. ὑπέσταν is corrected from ὑπέσσαν.
287 ἀπ' is corrected from ἐπ'.
288 ἐκπέρσαντ' is corrected from ἐκπέρσατ'.
289, 290 are omitted, but are added at foot of column.
292 θ' is corrected from δ'.
293 πολυζύγῳ is corrected from ὀιζύγῳ.
294 κειμέριαι for χειμέριαι.
295 ἡμῖν is corrected from ἡμεῖς. περιπροπέων for περιτροπέων.
298 κενεόν is corrected from καινεόν.
299 τλῆτε is corrected from τλῆται, and μείνατ' from μίμνατ'.

300 εἰ for ἦ. Κάλχας is corrected from Χάλκας.
301 τόδε, ἐστέ are corrected from τότε, ἔσται.
303 This line was mis-written at first into mere gibberish, but is corrected.
307 ῥέεν is corrected from νέεν.
309 δ' for ῥ'. Ὀλύμπιος is corrected from Ὀλύμπις.
311 νεοσσοί is corrected from νεοσοί.
313 τέκε is corrected from δέκα.
314 κατήσθιε is corrected from καταίσθιε. τετριγῶτας is wrongly altered to τετριγότας.
315 ὀδυρομένη is corrected from ὀδυρόμενα.
316 ἐλιξάμενος for ἐλελιξάμενος.
317 κατά is corrected from κα.
318 ἀρίζηλον for ἀίζηλον. ὅς is corrected from ὅ.
322 θεοπροπέων is corrected from θεοπρεπέων.
323 κομόωντες is corrected from κομόωντας.
324 μέν is corrected to μήν.
326 τέκν' ἔφαγεν for τέκνα φάγε.
328 τοσσαῦτ' ἔτεα is corrected from τοσαυτοτεα.
333 ἔφατ' is corrected from ἔφαθ'. μέγ' ἴαχον is corrected from μετίαχον.
335 ἐπαινήσαντες is corrected from ἐγενήσαντες.
337 ἀγοράασθε is corrected from ἠγοράασθε.
338 μέλει is corrected from μόλει.
346 φθινύθευν for φθινύθειν.
347 δ' is inserted above the line.
348 Ἄργοσδ' is corrected from Ἄργος.
350 κατανεῦσαι is corrected from κατανεῦσε.
353 φαίν[ων] is corrected from φήν[ας].
355 κατακοιμηθῆναι is corrected from κατακυμηθῆναι.
356 δ' is corrected from θ'.
358 ἐϋσσέλμοιο is corrected from ἐϋσέλμοιο.
361 οὔ τοι is corrected from αὐτοί, and ὅττι from ὅτι.
362 κατά is corrected from καὶ τά.
363 φῦλά τε φύλοις is corrected from φύλα τε φύλοις.

364 πείθωνται is corrected from πείθονται.
366 ὅς is corrected from ὅ, and μαχέονται from μαχέοντε.
367 καί is corrected from κε.
370 υἷας is corrected from υἷες.
373 δέ for κε. ἠμύσειε is corrected from ἠμύσει.
374 ἡμετέρῃσιν is corrected from ἡμετέρῃσι.
375 ἄλγε' ἔδωκεν is corrected from ἄλλα γε ἔθηκεν.
376 μέ is corrected from μέν.
378 ἀντιβίοις is corrected from ἀντιβίης. δ' is added above the line. χαλεπαίνων is corrected from ἐπέεσσιν.
380 ἔσσεται οὐδ' ἠβαιόν is corrected from ἔσσετ' οὐδὲ βαῖνον.
383 ὠκυπόδεσσιν is corrected from ὠκυπόροισιν.
384 πολέμοιο is corrected from πολέμο.
385 κε is corrected from κεν. πανημερίοις for πανημέριοι.
386 οὐδ' ἠβαιόν is corrected from οὐδὲ βαῖνον.
388 τευ τελαμών is corrected from δευτελαμ. στήθεσσιν (corrected from στήθεσιν) for στήθεσφιν.
391 ἐθέλοντα is corrected from αἰθέλοντα.
396 σκοπέλει for σκοπέλῳ.
399 κάπνισαν, corrected from κάπμισαν, for κάπνισσαν.
410 περιστήσαντο for περίστησάν τε.
415 θύρετρα is corrected from μέλαθρα.
419 ἐπεκράανε for ἐπεκραίαινε.
420 ἀμέγαρτον for ἀλίαστον.
421 εὔξαντο is corrected from εὔξοντο.
422 πρῶτα is corrected from πρῶτον, and ἔσφαξαν from ἔφασχαν.
423 τε is corrected from δέ.
427 μῆρ' ἐκάη for μῆρα κάη.
428 μίστυλον δ' for μίστυλλόν τ'.
435 αὖθι is corrected from αὐτά.
436 ἀμβαλλώμεθα is corrected from ἀμβαλώμεθα.
462 ἀγαλλόμαναι for ἀγαλλόμενα.
463 τε is corrected from ται.
467 ἵσταν is corrected from ἔνσταν.

470 ἱλάσκονται for ἡλάσκουσιν.
471 εἰαρεινῆ for εἰαρινῆ. δέ for τε. γλάγος is corrected from γλάκος.
474 τ' is added above the line.
479 τε for the first δέ.
480 ἔξοχος is corrected from ἔχος.
481 τε is inserted in another hand.
483 ἐκπρεπέ' is corrected in another hand from ἐκπρε.
490 ἄρρηκτος is corrected from ἄρηκτος.
491 κοῦραι is inserted after μοῦσαι.

The book ends with l. 493. The end is marked by the usual flourish, and by the inscription τέλος ἔχει Ἰλιάδος [β] ᾱ β̄ γ̄ δ̄..., after which is written the number of lines in the final column, λϛ̄, =36. The next book is begun on a fresh column.

Il. iii. 12 τις for τίς τ'. λεύσει for λεύσσει.
13 ποσσί is corrected from ποσί.
28 τίσασθαι for τίσεσθαι.
34 ἐμ βήσῃς for ἐν βήσσῃς.
40 ὄφελος for ὄφελες. ἔμμεναι for ἔμεναι.
42 ἔμμεναι for ἔμεναι.
50 πόλεϊ for πόληι.
57 εἶσο for ἔσσο.
62 ὀφέλει for ὀφέλλει.
68 Τρῶας κάθιζον for κάθισον Τρῶας.
71 καί for κε. τε is corrected from ται.
74 ναίοιτε is corrected from ναίοιμεν.
76 ἔφατ' for ἔφαθ'.
77 μέσον for μέσσον.
78 μέσου for μέσσου. ἰδρύθησαν for ἰδρύνθησαν.
82 εἴσχεσθ' for ἴσχεσθ'. βάλλετε is corrected from βάλλεται.
92 καί for κε.
94 is omitted. The omission is indicated by a mark in the margin, and the line was probably supplied at the

bottom of the column, where there are some faint traces of writing.
98 διακριθήμεναι for διακρινθήμεναι.
101 ὁπποτέρων for ὁπποτέρῳ.
102 διακριθεῖτε, corrected from διακριθεῖται, for διακρινθεῖτε.
103 οἴσετε, apparently corrected from οἴσετ', for οἴσετε δ'. ἑταίρην for ἑτέρην.
104 τ' for δ'.
105 ἕξετε for ἄξετε.
114 ἐκδύοντο for ἐξεδύοντο. κατέθεντ' is corrected from κατέθενδ'.
119 ἄρν' ἐκέλευεν for ἄρνα κέλευεν.
121 λευκωλεύνῳ for λευκωλένῳ.
126 μαρμαρέην for πορφυρέην. ἀνέπασσεν for ἐνέπασσεν.
127 Ἀκαιῶν for Ἀχαιῶν.
128 ἕθεν is corrected from ἕνεκ'.
132 ἀλλήλοισιν for ἀλλήλοισι.
137 ἐγχείησιν for ἐγχείῃσι.
138 καί for κε. κεκλήσῃ is corrected from καικλήσῃ.
146 Θυμήτην for Θυμοίτην.
147 Κλυθίον for Κλυτίον.
151 τεττίγεσσιν is corrected from τεττίγεσιν.
152 ἵησαν (apparently), corrected from ἵεσαν, for ἱεῖσιν.
153 ἦντ' is corrected from ἦνδ'.
154 ἴδον for εἴδονθ'.
160 τεκέεσσί τ' is corrected from τεκέεσσιν.
163 ἴδης for ἴδῃ.
164 νῦν for νύ.
165 Ἀχαιῶν is corrected from Ἄργος.
169 οὔπω was omitted originally, and is added later.
170 οὔπω for οὕτω. γεραρόν is corrected from γεραόν.
172 αἰδοῖος is corrected from ἀίδιος.
176 κλείουσα for κλαίουσα.
178 γ' is omitted.
187 Σαγγαρίοιο is corrected from ἀγγαρίοιο.

188 ἐγών is corrected from ἐών.
190 τόσσοι for τόσοι. ἑλικώπιδες for ἑλίκωπες.
195 πουλυβοτείρῃ is corrected from πολυβοτείρῃ.
196 ἐπεπωλεῖτο for ἐπιπωλεῖται.
197 πηγεσιμάλλῳ is corrected from πηγεσίμαλλον.
199 ἐκγεγαγυῖα for ἐκγεγαυῖα.
205 ἤλυθεν for ἦλυθε.
207 μεγάροις ἐφίλησα for μεγάροισι φίλησα.
212 ὅτε is corrected from ὅδε, and μύθους from μύθου.
214 οὐ is added later above the line, and πολύμυθος is corrected from πολύμηθος.
215 ἦ is corrected to εἰ.
217 στάσκεν is corrected from στάνκεν.
218 προπηνές for προπρηνές.
219 ἀιδρεϊ is corrected from ἀιδρι.
223 ἐρείσειεν for ἐρίσσειε.
224 ἀγασσάμεσθ' for ἀγασσάμεθ'.
227 ἠδ' for τε καί.
230 Κρήτεσσι is corrected from Θρήκεσσι.
231 ἠερέθονται for ἠγερέθονται.
234 ἑλίκωπας is corrected in another hand from καὶ πάντας.
235 is omitted, and is added in another hand at the top of the column.
239 ἐπέσθην, corrected from ἐπέσχην, for ἐσπέσθην.
250 ὄρσε for ὄρσεο.
257 νέονται is corrected from νεέσθων.
259 ἑταίρους for ἑταίροις.
260 ἐπείθοντο for ἐπίθοντο.
264 ἵκανον for ἵκοντο.
265 πολυβότειραν for πουλυβότειραν.
266 μέσον for μέσσον.
267 δ' is added above the line.
272 is omitted and is added in another hand at the top of the column.
273 τάμεν for τάμνε.

274 νεῖμεν for νεῖμαν.
277 ἐφορᾷς is corrected to ἐφορᾷ. ἐπακούει for ἐπακούεις.
278 οἴ is omitted. καμόντας is corrected to καμόντες.
282 κτήματα πάντα has been altered, apparently to κτήματ' ἄμ' αὐτῇ, but both correction and original text have been struck out.
289 ἐθέλουσιν for ἐθέλωσιν.
291 κε is corrected from καί.
295 ἀφυσσάμενοι for ἀφυσσόμενοι.
302 ἔφατ' for ἔφαν. ἐπεκράανε for ἐπεκραίαινε.
306 τλήσσομ' for τλήσομ'.
308 τόδε for τό γε.
310 εἰς for ἐς.
323 δ' is omitted.
326 ἑκάστῳ for ἑκάστου.
328 ἐδύσατο for ἐδύσετο.
330 πρῶτα is corrected from πρῶτον.
332 στήθεσσιν is corrected from σθήθεσσιν.
339 δ' is omitted.
341 μέσον for μέσσον.
345 σεῖον δ' for σείοντ'. ἀλλήλοισι κοτέοντες for ἀλλήλοισιν κοτέοντε.
348 χαλκόν for χαλκός.
349 ἀσπίδι ἐν for ἀσπίδ' ἐνί.
352 ἐμαῖς for ἐμῆς.
355 ἀμπεπαλών is corrected from ἀμπεπαρών.
357 ὄμβριμον for ὄβριμον.
358 θώρηκτος for θώρηκος.
359 ἀντικρύ for ἀντικρύς. δέ is added above the line.
360 ἐκλίνθη is corrected from ἐνκλίνθη.
367 ἐν is corrected from ἐγ.
369 λάβεν is corrected from φάλον.
370 εἷλκε for ἕλκε.
371 ἀπαλὴν ὑπό is corrected from ἀπαλῆς ἀπό (the termination of δειρήν is wanting in the MS.).

373 εἴρυσεν for εἴρυσσεν.
377 ἔπειτ' for ἔπειθ'.
379 ἐπόρουσαι for ἐπόρουσε.
387 ναιεταώσῃ for ναιετοώσῃ.
388 φιλέεσκεν is corrected from καλέεσκεν.
392 ἵμασιν for εἵμασιν.
393 μαχεσσάμενον for μαχησάμενον. τόνδ' for τόν γ'.
396 ῥ' is added above the line.
398 δ' for the first τ'.
400 προτέρων for προτέρω.
402 κακεῖθει for καὶ κεῖθι.
404 οἴκαδ' is corrected from οἴκον.
405 is omitted, and is added at the head of the column.
406 ἀπόειπε for ἀπόεικε. It is possible that a ϛ is lost after κελεύθου.
415 ἔκπαγλ' ἐφίλησα for ἔκπαγλα φίλησα.
417 Δαναῶν is corrected from δαῶν.
418 ἔφαθ' for ἔφατ'. ἔδδεισεν for ἔδεισεν. δ' is omitted. ἐγγεγαυῖα for ἐκγεγαυῖα.
424 φιλομειδής for φιλομμειδής.
428 πολέμοιο for πολέμου.
436 δαμάσθης for δαμήης.
438 ὀνείδεσιν for ὀνείδεσι. ἔνισπε for ἔνιπτε.
440 εἰσί is corrected from εἰ.
442 ὧδε ἔρως, corrected from ὧδ' ἔρως, for ὧδε γ' ἔρος.
446 ὡσέο for ὡς σέο.
447 ἄρχε for ἦρχε. τ' for δ'.
451 δ' for τ'.
453 γ' is omitted. ἐκεύθανεν for ἐκεύθανον.
460 ἐσσομένοισιν for ἐσσομένοισι.
461 ἔφαθ' for ἔφατ'. Ἀτρείδης is added above the line.

At the end of the book is the inscription τέλος ἔχει Ἰλιάδος γ̄.

IL. IV. 2 τε is inserted after δαπέδῳ.
 10 φιλομειδής for φιλομμειδής.

17 αὔτως for αὖ πως.
19 δ' is omitted.
20 ἐπέμοιξαν for ἐπέμυξαν.
29 ἔρδε for ἔρδ'.
33 Ἰλίου for Ἴλιον. ἐυκτείμενον for ἐυκτίμενον.

PLATE VII.

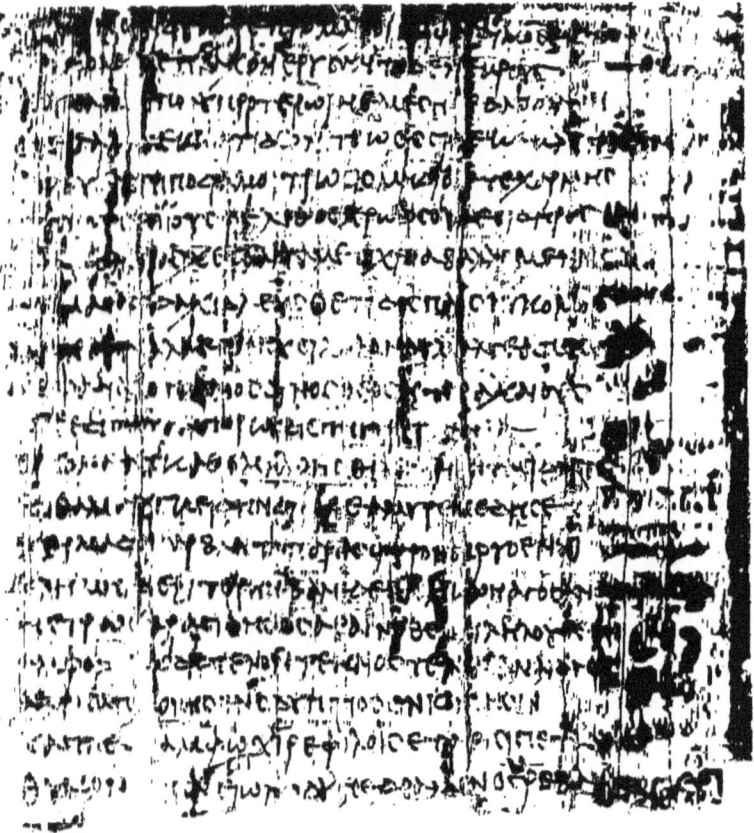

ΟΜΗΡΟΥ ΙΛΙΑΔΟΣ

Γ Δ

Papyrus CXXXVI verso.

THE *recto* of this papyrus contains some accounts; but the *verso* of it has been used to receive the third and fourth books of the Iliad. The portion containing the third book is lost, with the exception of some fragments of two columns; but the greater part of the fourth book has survived. The latter was written in twelve columns, and the last five of these are almost perfect, while there are considerable remains of every other column except the first two, of which only small fragments are preserved. At the end of the roll, as it was acquired by the Museum, is an additional piece of papyrus, mostly blank, but containing some large characters, which are almost obliterated; but the writing on the *recto* of this piece shows that it did not originally belong to the same papyrus as the rest. The portion of papyrus containing the fourth book would have measured, when intact, about five feet in length, and its height, which is unusually great, is just over 12 inches. The number of lines in a column vary from 63 (in the first column, which is in a different hand from the rest) to 42, not reckoning the final column, which only contains 17 lines; but the ordinary number is about 46. There are two hands employed in the MS., but one of them is confined to the first column of the fourth book, of which there are only a few small remnants. The hand in which the bulk of the MS. is written is a rough, ugly uncial of medium size, which does not suggest much culture on the part of the scribe. This impression is confirmed by the orthography and the state of the text. The common interchange of ει and ι is carried to considerable lengths, υ is more than once substituted for οι, κ is twice written for γ, the ι adscript is repeatedly added in wrong places, and obvious mistakes are far from uncommon. Corrections are sometimes made by the original scribe, sometimes in a different hand and fainter ink. The result is a somewhat indifferent representation of the vulgate text, and there is hardly a single variant which deserves consideration.

The number of lines in each column is stated at its foot, and the hundreds were also indicated in the margin. Of the latter numeration only one instance remains, the letter δ, enclosed in a flourish, being placed opposite l. 404, which appears to prove that four lines of our text were wanting in the MS.; but there is no indication in the extant remains to show which these were. There are no accents or breathings, but dots are occasionally used to indicate pauses in the sense, either at the ends or in the middle of lines. In the latter case the dot is placed above the end of the word with which the sense closes, not in the line of writing.

As regards the date of the MS., the writing is of a comparatively late type, and may perhaps be ascribed to the third century of our era. The accounts on the *recto* are not dated, but they appear to belong to the latter part of the second century, and it is not probable that the Homer was inscribed on the *verso* at a very much later date.

The following is a table of the lines which appear in the surviving portions of the MS. As far as IV. 352 inclusive the lines are in no place complete, but are represented by fragments more or less large; in the remainder of the book the MS. is for the most part intact.

III. 317–337	IV. 159–192
345–372	198–201
IV. 1–28	208–245
56–69	256–293
74–79	303–345
111–150	352–544

The columns of the MS. begin with the following lines: III. 317, 365, IV. 1, 64, 111, 159, 208, 256, 303, 353, 399, 443, 487, 529. At the end of the fourth book, after a short blank interval, is written the first line of the fifth book, to indicate the proper succession; and this is followed by the title 'Ἰλιάδος δ'.

The autotype plate is taken from the eleventh column of the fourth book, containing ll. 505–524.

Il. III.   326 ἑκάστῳ for ἑκάστου.
           327 ἔκειτο is written as a correction, but the original word is obliterated, except the termination—ου.
IV.   15 ῥ' is omitted.
           20 ἔφατ' for ἔφαθ'.

ΙΛΙΑΔΟΣ Δ.   95

23 σχυζομένη for σκυζομένη.
61 κέκληται for κέκλημαι.
62 ταῦτ' for ταῦθ'.
63 σοί for σύ.
68 ὡς φάτ[ο] for ὡς ἔφατ'.
114 ἀπαΐξειαν (corrected from -ειεν) for ἀναΐξειαν.
116 ἐγ for ἐκ.
118 κατεκόσμει (corrected from κατὰ κόσμου) for κατεκόσμεε.
119 εὔχετο is corrected from εὔχεο.
129 ἐχεπευχές for ἐχεπευκές.
161 ἀπέτισαν is corrected from ἀνέτισαν.
166 σφίν for σφί.
170 μ[οῖραν] for πότμον.
174 ἄρουραν for ἄρουρα.
175 κειμένῳ for κειμένου.
179 ὥς κέν οἱ for ὡς καὶ νῦν.
181 νευσί for νηυσί.
185 καιρείῳ for καιρίῳ.
213 δέ for δ' ἐκ.
219 ποτέ for πόρε.
228 Πολ[εμαίου] for Πτολεμαίου.
259 δαιτί for δαίθ'.
263 ἀνώγοι for ἀνώγῃ.
265 εὖδα for ηὖδα.
268 ὄτρυνε is corrected from ὤτρυνε.
275 σκοπιῆς is corrected from σκοπιήν.
283 [καὶ μ]ὲν τούς for καὶ τοὺς μέν.
303 ἱπποσύνῃσι for ἱπποσύνῃ τε.
307 ἐπεί is corrected from ἐπί.
308 πολέας for πόλιας.
312 προσεύδα for προσηύδα.
318 κεν for τοι.
321 ἱκάνει for ὀπάζει.
323 θανόντων for γερόντων.
327 πλήθιππον for πλήξιππον.

339 λόγοισι for δόλοισι.
353 ἤν κ' for ἤν.
359 νεικείωι ... κελεύωι for νεικείω ... κελεύω.
363 μεταμώλια for μεταμώνια. θεῖεν is corrected from θεῖον, in later hand.
367 εἱστήκει for ἑστήκει.
368 καὶ μὲν τόν for καὶ τὸν μέν.
369 προσεύδα for προσηύδα.
371 ὀπείπενες for ὀπιπεύεις.
372 πτωσσκαζέμεν for πτωσκαζέμεν.
378 δέ for ῥα.
379 μαλίσσοντο for μάλα λίσσοντο.
382 ὁτοῦ for ὁδοῦ.
395 Λυκοφόντης for Πολυφόντης.
397 νέεσθαι is corrected from νέαισθαι.
398 Μαίον' is corrected from Μαίων'. ἀναπροέηκε for ἄρα προέηκε.
400 ἀμείνωι for ἀμείνων.
402 βασιλῆος is corrected from βασιλῆες.
410 A mark (>) is placed against this line in the margin. ὁμοίη is corrected from ὅμοιον.
412 σιωπῇ is corrected from σιοπῇ.
418 ἄρα for ἄγε.
424 κορύσσεται is corrected from κορέσσεται.
426 ἐόν for ἰόν.
427 ὤρνυντο for κίνυντο.
431 δειδιότας for δειδιότες.
434 ἑστήκωσιν for ἑστήκασιν.
435 μεμακυῖαι is corrected from μεμανῖαι.
438 ἔσαν is corrected in later hand from ἔσεν.
439 κλαυκῶπις for γλαυκῶπις.
449 ὀρυμακδός for ὀρυμαγδός.
455 τῶν δ' ὅτε (corrected from ὡς δ' ὅτε) for τῶν δέ τε. δοῦπος for δοῦπον.
456 φόβος for πόνος.

458 Θαλυσιάδην is corrected from Θαλοισιάδην.
461 is omitted.
472 ἀλλήλους for ἀλλήλοις. ἐπόρουσαν is corrected from ἐπόρουσεν.
490 Πριαμείδης for Πριαμίδης.
494 Ὀδυσσεύς for Ὀδυσεύς, and so in l. 501.
498 ἀκοντίσαντος for ἀκοντίσσαντος.
506 μέγ' εἴαχον for μέγα ἴαχον.
510 Ἀργείους for Ἀργείοις. σφί is corrected from σφέ. χρωὸς οὐδέ for χρὼς οὔτε.
512 Ἀχιλλεύς for Ἀχιλεύς.
513 νευσί for νηυσί.
517 μῦρ' ἐπέδησε for μοῖρα πέδησεν.
518 ὀκρυόεντι for ὀκριόεντι.
520 Πείρως for Πείροος.
524 ὑπέδραμεν for ἐπέδραμεν.
527 ἐπεσσύμενον for ἀπεσσύμενον.
542 ἐλοῦσ' αὐτάρ for ἐλοῦσα ἀτάρ.

ΟΜΗΡΟΥ ΙΛΙΑΔΟΣ

Ε Ζ Σ

Papyrus CXXVII.

UNDER this number are included several small fragments of the eighteenth book of the Iliad, together with a few of the fifth and sixth. In no case is a complete line preserved, and in only one instance is any large part of a column intact (*viz.* that which contains the end of Book XVIII.). With this one exception the fragments are all extremely small; and, as a natural consequence, their evidence is not important. The MS. of the eighteenth book was originally written on a roll containing fourteen columns, each measuring about 5 in. in width, while the height of the papyrus is 10 in. Each column contained as a rule 45 lines. The hand is an upright and rather square uncial of fair size, and accents and marks of elision are added, apparently in the original hand. The ι adscript is generally omitted, but not always. The MS. has all the appearance of a comparatively late date, and may perhaps be ascribed to the third or fourth century. The lines are marked off by hundreds, as appears from the letter α prefixed to l. 100, and ε to l. 505. The latter indicates that five lines of our present text were omitted in this MS., and as it appears that the second column contained ll. 46–91, the sixth and seventh ll. 227–319, and the ninth ll. 366–411, which brings them above the normal number of forty-five lines to the column, it is possible that ll. 49, 300–2, and 381 were omitted.

The fragments of the fifth and sixth books are few and insignificant. Those of the fifth book are written in a semi-cursive hand, the letters leaning somewhat to the left; while those of the sixth are uncial, the letters being rather taller and finer than the characters in which the MS. of the eighteenth book is written.

The following is a list of the passages contained in these MSS.; but each line named is only represented by a fragment, and generally a small one.

ΟΜΗΡΟΥ ΙΛΙΑΔΟΣ Ε, Ζ, Σ.

Il. V.	731-734	Il. XVIII.	279-288
	815-818		320-349
	846-850		359-371
VI.	90-100		387-394
	119-125		398-410
XVIII.	1-22		412-425
	29-33		442-450
	77-92		455-465
	98-121		467-477
	125-136		479-492
	152-161		501-518
	168-175		534-543
	227-230		563-575
	273-275		578-617

The text is correctly written, so far as can be gathered from these fragments, and the variants are not of much importance. The reading ἐς in l. 565 confirms the text of Zenodotus, of which Didymus approved.

It has not been thought worth while to give a facsimile of these fragments.

Il. xviii. 14 [ἐπὶ ν]ῆας ἴναι for ἐπὶ νῆας ἴμεν.
15 ἕως for εἶος.
100 Opposite this line is the character ᾱ in the margin.
227 'Αθήνῃ for 'Αθήνη.
350 is written at the bottom of the column, after l. 365, and therefore was presumably omitted in its proper place.
505 Opposite this line is the character ε̄ in the margin.
537 is omitted in text and added at foot of column. τεθ-νειῶτα for τεθνηῶτα.
565 ἐς for ἐπ'.
580 μεμηκώς for μεμυκώς.
584 ὀτρύναντες for ὀτρύνοντες.
591 Κνωσσῷ for Κνωσῷ.
601 θέλῃσι for θέῃσιν.

Part of the title of the book is visible at the end.

ΟΜΗΡΟΥ ΙΛΙΑΔΟΣ

Ψ   Ω

Papyrus CXXVIII.

This papyrus contains very considerable fragments of the last two books of the Iliad. With the exception of one large lacuna in book XXIII. there are fragments of almost every column, so that it is possible to estimate with sufficient accuracy the original dimensions of the MS. It was a roll of about 20 ft. in length and 9? in. in height, written in 43 or 44 columns, of which 23 contained the text of book XXIII., and 20 (with possibly a small portion of a 21st) that of book XXIV. The number of lines to a column is, as a rule, forty. The text is written in one hand throughout, except in one place, where it is evident that a column (the first of book XXIV.) had been torn off, together with the ends of the lines of the preceding column. Both the missing column and the final letters of its predecessor have been supplied by a different scribe, but the work has been done with extreme negligence or ignorance, and this part of the text is full of blunders and is practically valueless. The rest of the MS. is written in an uncial hand of a fair size, very clear and not ungraceful, and of a decidedly early type. The columns lean to the right, and changes of speakers are indicated by the horizontal strokes between the beginnings of lines, which have already been noticed in the Hyperides and Demosthenes. The hundreds are indicated by numerals in the margin; but these only remain in four cases, opposite XXIII. 502, 604, 705, 805. From this numeration it is clear that certain lines in our vulgate were wanting in the MS. The two missing before l. 502 were probably either ll. 92 and 701 or ll. 405, 6, all of which were athetised by Aristarchus; l. 565 was certainly omitted, but no other has dropped out between ll. 502 and 604, so the numeration is either wrong or else is taken from a MS. which omitted also l. 581 (athetised by Aristarchus); between ll. 604 and 705 l. 626 was omitted; and between ll. 705 and 805 l. 804

ΟΜΗΡΟΥ ΙΛΙΑΔΟΣ Ψ, Ω.

is omitted in the text, but not in the numeration. At the end of book XXIII. the total number of lines in the book is given as 890, whereas the total in our text is 897. Pauses in the sense are marked by punctuation, dots being placed either at the ends of lines or above the last word of a clause in the middle of lines; but these appear not to be in the original hand. The ι adscript is regularly written. The only common variation in spelling is the familiar one of substituting ει for ι. Breathings, accents, and marks of elision are entirely absent from the original MS., but they have been added freely by a later hand, probably the same as that to which the punctuation is due. Corrections of obvious errors have also been made in a later hand throughout. The MS. must certainly be classed among the earliest of the Homer papyri that have yet been discovered, and may probably be assigned to the first century B.C.

Apart from a certain number of obvious scribe's blunders, from which no MS. (and particularly no papyrus MS.) is free, the text is well written, and forms a good reproduction of the vulgate. In some cases it adds a witness to readings of Aristarchus, as to which there has hitherto been some doubt, as in the omission of XXIII. 626, and in the spelling παλαιμοσύνης in XXIII. 701. But the chief interest of this MS. lies in the occurrence in it of the critical symbols employed by Aristarchus. Hitherto the earliest extant document in which they have been known is a papyrus in the Bodleian library at Oxford, which is ascribed to the 5th century of our era. The present MS. carries back the tradition some five hundred years earlier, though it does not really increase the knowledge which we already possess concerning them from the scholia. In many places the margins of the columns have been lost, so that it is impossible to say whether the critical signs were present or not; but also in many places in which the margins are intact the signs are not given where we know, from other sources, that they should have occurred. The use of them is, in fact, rare, and is almost confined to the διπλῆ (≻), which is the sign of reference to notes on grammar, matter, &c. This is prefixed to XXIII. 486, 550, 551, 574, 680 (should be 679), 850, 863, 872, XXIV. 228, 232, 544. The asterisk (indicating that the line occurs elsewhere in Homer) is found before XXIII. 657.

A few scholia are written in a small and rather difficult hand, but in every case they are mutilated.

A list is here given of the passages contained in these fragments. Of the 23 columns in which book XXIII. was written, we have parts of all except the eight which contained ll. 79–401; and of the 20 columns of book XXIV. portions (often extremely small) remain of all except the eighth, which contained ll. 283–322, and the last, which contained ll. 760–804. But in no case (except the extremely corrupt first column of book XXIV. mentioned above) is any column complete, and in many instances lines included in the following list are represented only by one or two letters.

XXIII.	1-79	XXIV.	344-351
	402-633		382-387
	638-814		402-479
	823-897		490-520
			536-548
XXIV.	1-83		559-577
	100-158		596-611
	164-243		631-657
	248-274		672-728
	276-282		737-744
	337-341		754-759

The columns of the MS. begin with the following lines:—XXIII. 1, 40, 402, 441, 480, 519, 558, 598, 638, 677, 717, 756, 796, 836, 878, XXIV. 1, 41, 81, 122, 164, 204, 244, 283, [323, 362, 401], 441, 479, 521, 563, 602, 641, 680, 721, 760.

The autotype plate is taken from the 12th column of book XXIII. and contains ll. 441-461 of that book.

Il. xxiii. 39 Omitted (between end of first column and beginning of second), and supplied in smaller and rougher hand.
40 τρίποδαν for τρίποδα.
42 γ' om.
45 γε is corrected from τε.
48 πειθώμεθα is corrected to τερπώμεθα.
50 ὡς for ὅσσ'.
61 ἀπ' for ἐπ'.
72 με εἴργουσι for μ' ἐέργουσι.
76 [ν]είομαι for νίσσομαι.
407 λίπησθε for λίπησθον.
417 ὑποδδείσαντες for ὑποδείσαντες.
418 ἐπιδραμέτην for ἐπεδραμέτην.
425 ἔδδεισε for ἔδεισε, and so elsewhere.
427 παρελάσσαι for παρελάσσεις.

ΙΛΙΑΔΟΣ Ψ.

433 ἐπιδραμέτην for ἐπεδραμέτην.
434 ἐλαύνειν is corrected from ἐλαύνων.
435 συνκύρσειαν for συγκύρσειαν, and similarly elsewhere.
444 καμόντε for καμόντα.
449 οἱ for τοί.
451 ἐν is corrected from ἦν.
452 ἰόντος for ἐόντος. ἀκούων for ἀκούσας.
464 ἄν for ἄμ.
472 ἱπποδάμου is corrected from ἱπποτάμου.
483 νείκει for νεῖκος.
485 περιδώμεθον for περιδώμεθα.
486 has the διπλῆ.
490 τι for δή.
492 ἀμείβεσθον is corrected from ἀμείβεσθαι.
497 γνώσεσθε is corrected from γνώσεσθαι.
498 τό for τε.
547 τό κεν for τῷ κ'.
550 has the διπλῆ. τοι corrected from οἱ.
551 has the διπλῆ.
565 is omitted.
568 χερσί for χειρί.
574 has the διπλῆ.
593 ἀπαιτήσειας for ἐπαιτήσειας.
598 A little space above this line, which begins a column, are the words (in a different hand) ἆ δὴ ταῦτα . . .
599 φρίσσωσιν for φρίσσουσιν.
600 τοι for σοί.
602 κεν for τοι.
605 ἀμείμονας for ἀμείνονας. ἠπεροπεύειν is corrected from ἠπεροπεύει.
607 πόλλ' ἔπαθες καὶ πόλλ' ἐμόγησας for πολλὰ πάθες καὶ πολλὰ μόγησας.
626 is omitted.
639 βαλόντες for βαλόντε. ἀγασσάμενοι for ἀγασσαμένω.
641 ἡνιόχευεν is corrected from ἡνιέχευεν.
642 μάστιγι is corrected from μάστιγα.

648 ἀεί is corrected to αἰεί.
649 τε is corrected from τό.
657 has the asterisk. Ἀργείοισιν is corrected from ἀνθρώποισιν.
662 φερέσθω for νεέσθω.
674 κηδεμόνες is corrected from κηδομόνες.
678 Μηκιστέως for Μηκιστῆος.
679 Θήβας for Θήβασδ'.
680 has the διπλῆ.
682 μάλα for μέγα.
691 εἰστήκει for ἑστήκειν.
693 θεινί for θίν'. φοικιόεντι for φυκιόεντι. τε for δέ. κῦμ' ἐκάλυψεν for κῦμα κάλυψεν.
701 παλαιμοσύνης for παλαισμοσύνης.
707 πειρήσεσθε for πειρήσεσθον.
709 Ὀδυσσεύς for Ὀδυσεύς, and so elsewhere; similarly with the name Ἀχιλλεύς.
721 ἐυκνήμιδες Ἀχαιοί for ἐυκνήμιδας Ἀχαιούς.
726 κώληπα is corrected from πήληκα.
727 ἔβαλ' for ἔπεσ'.
732 πλησίον for πλησίοι.
736 ἴσ' is corrected from εἰσ.
739 ἀπομορξάμενοι for ἀπομορξαμένω.
751 ἔθηκεν is corrected from ἔθικεν.
753 πειρήσεσθον for πειρήσεσθε.
757 After this line is a mark of omission, and at the head of the column are written lines 359-361: l. 358 is identical with l. 757, which is, no doubt, the cause of this insertion. Perhaps these additional lines were the cause of Aristarchus' *obelus* to l. 757.
759 Ὀδυσσεύς is corrected from Ἐπειός.
761 χειρί for χερσί.
767 ἱέμενοι for ἱεμένῳ.
770 κλῦθι is corrected from κῦθι.
773 ἔμελλεν for ἔμελλον.

782 φίλοι for πόποι.
785 δή is added above the line.
804 is omitted.
817 ἐπήιξαν is corrected from [ἐπή]ιξεν.
848 ἀνστάντες is corrected from ἀστάντες.
850 has the διπλῆ. σίδηρον: there is a gloss in the margin, but mutilated, σεσημείωτ[αι] .. σίδηρον ..
854 ἧς is corrected from ἡ.
863 has the διπλῆ.
864 is omitted.
867 ἀντικρύ for ἀντικρύς, and so in l. 876.
871 ἔχεν is corrected from ἔχον.
872 has the διπλῆ.
874 ὑπαί for ὑπό.
875 μέσσην is corrected from μέσσον.
879 λιάσθη for λίασθεν: the last letters of each line in this column have been supplied by the writer of the following column, who is not to be trusted.
882 ἀέθλους for ἄειρεν.
885 ἀνθεμόεντος for ἀνθεμόεντα.
888 Ἰδομενῆας for Ἰδομενῆος.
892 is omitted, but is supplied at the foot of the column, and the note κάτω is written opposite its proper place.
896 γ' ἥρως is a correction; the original reading is mostly obliterated, but it ended in -σεν.
897 ἄεθλα for ἄεθλον.

The end of the book is followed by its title and the number of lines contained in it, but only a part of this inscription remains

[τέλος ἔχει]
[Ἰλιά]δος
[Ψ]
[ΙΙΙΙΙΙΙΙΙΙΙ]ΙΙΙΠΔΔΔ

IL. XXIV. 1 θεάς for θοάς.
4 κλέε for κλαῖε.

6 ἀνανδροτῆτα for ἀδροτῆτα.
7 καί is corrected from παι.
8 δέ for the first τε.
9 μεμνησκόμενος for μιμνησκόμενος.
10 κατακείμενον for κατακείμενος.
11 πρηνή for πρηνής.
13 ἠόνας for ἠιόνας.
17 ἐν for ἐνί. δ' for τ'.
19 φῶτα λεαίρων for φῶτ' ἐλεαίρων.
20 τεθνιότα for τεθνηότα. αἰγίτι for αἰγίδι.
21 χρυσίην for χρυσείη. ἀποτρύφυ for ἀποδρύφοι.
22 ἀεικείζει for ἀείκιζεν.
23 ἐλεαίρεσκεν for ἐλεαίρεσκον.
24 ὀτρύνεσκεν for ὀτρύνεσκον.
25 ἔνθ' ἄλλοι μὲν πάντες ἐπευφήμησαν Ἀχαιοί for ἔνθ' ἄλλοις μὲν πᾶσιν ἐήνδανεν, οὐδέ ποθ' Ἥρῃ.
26 ὀδέ for second οὐδέ.
27 ὥσφιν for ὥς σφιν.
28 ἀρχ[ῆς] for ἄτης.
29 νίκεσε for νείκεσσε. μέσαυχον for μέσσαυλον.
30 πόρε is corrected from πρό.
31 δυοδεκάτην for δυωδεκάτη.
33 ἐσθέ for ἐστέ. οὐ νε καί for οὔ νύ ποθ'.
34 Ἕκτωρα for Ἕκτωρ. ἐγῶν for αἰγῶν. τελίων for τελείων.
35 ἔτλη κε for ἔτλητε. ἐόντε for ἐόντα.
36 εἰδέειν for ἰδέειν.
37 Πριάμοιο for Πριάμῳ.
38 πι for ἐπί. κτέρα for κτέρεα. κτερέουσιν for κτερίσαιεν.
39 ἀλλοῷ for ἀλλ' ὀλοῷ. Ἀχιλλῆα for Ἀχιλῆι. βούλεσθαι παρήγειν for βούλεσθ' ἐπαρήγειν.
40 φρένας for φρένες. ἐναίσιμα for ἐναίσιμοι. οὐδέ for οὔτε.
47 The second ἠέ is corrected from ἤ.
48 ὀδυρόμενος for ὀδυράμενος.
53 νεμεσσηθῶμεν for νεμεσσηθέωμεν.
62 πάντες is corrected from πάντας.

ΙΛΙΑΔΟΣ Ω.

75 οἱ is added above the line.
76 θ' is corrected from τ'.
79 ἐπεστενάχιζε for ἐπεστονάχησε.
119 is omitted.
124 ἄριστον is corrected from ἄριστα.
126 παρέζετο for καθέζετο.
165 κατεμήσατο for καταμήσατο.
166 ἰδέ is corrected from ἰδέν.
172 ὀσσομένη is corrected from ὀσομένη.
177 οἷος for οἷον.
179 ηκε for ἠδέ.
191 κατεβήσατο for κατεβήσετο.
192 ...ονδει for κεχάνδει.
198 ἀνώγει for ἄνωγεν.
201 οἴχοντ' for οἴχονθ'.
202 ἄνασσες for ἀνάσσεις.
210 γεινομένῳ is corrected from γινομένῳ.
215 πρός for πρό.
219 ἐνιμμεγάροισι for ἐνὶ μεγάροισι.
228 has the διπλῆ.
231 καλά for λευκά. τόσσους for τόσους.
232 has the διπλῆ.
240 ὅτε for ὅτι. κηδήσοντες is corrected from κηδήσαντες.
265 πάντες for πατρός.
267 πρωτοπαγέα for πρωτοπαγῆ.
268 πασσαλόφιν for πασσαλόφι.
279 ὕπαγε for ὕπαγον.
340 ἔπειτ' for ἔπειθ'.
387 [ἀνθ]ρώπων for τοκήων.
417 [φαν]είη for φανήῃ.
422 ἐῆος for ἑοῖο.
436 γένηται for γένοιτο.
440 is omitted (between end of one column and the beginning of the next).
456 ἐπιρήσεσκε for ἐπιρρήσεσκε.

467 ἵνα is corrected from ἵν'.
501 εἵνεκ' for εἵνεχ'.
515 αὐτίκα δ' ἐκ for αὐτίκ' ἀπό.
518 ἄσχεο for ἄνσχεο.
519, 520 are omitted between two columns, but supplied in later hand.
544 has the διπλῆ.
565 κεν for κε.
566 οὔτε for first οὐδέ. ὀχῆας for ὀχῆα.
567 πυλάων for θυράων.
568 τῶ νῦν is corrected from τῶν.
571 ... γησεν for ἔδεισεν. Prob. ὣς φάτ' ἐσίγησεν κ.τ.λ.
608 γείνατο is corrected from γίνατο.
646 ἔσασθαι is corrected from ἔσεσθαι.
648 δοιώ is corrected from δύω. ἐγκονέουσαι is corrected from ἐγκαι[έουσαι].
678 εὗδον is corrected from ηὗδον.
681 πυλαουρούς for πυλαωρούς.
693 is omitted.
697 ἄγον for φέρον.
699 χρυσέῃ is corrected from χρυσῇ.
704 Ἕκτορα δῖο[ν] for Ἕκτορ' ἰόντες.
707 ... η τις for οὐδέ τις αὐτόθ'.
717 ἀγάγοιμι for ἀγάγωμι.
721 θρήνους for θρήνων.
722 ἄρ' ἐθρήνε[ον] for δὴ θρήνεον.
724 ἱπποδάμ[οιο] for ἀνδροφόνοιο.

PLATE IX.

ΤΡΥΦΩΝΟΣ

ΤΕΧΝΗ ΓΡΑΜΜΑΤΙΚΗ.

Papyrus CXXVI verso.

It has already been mentioned in the introduction to Papyrus CXXVI *recto* (above, p. 81) that three of the blank pages in that manuscript had been used to receive the text of a grammatical work bearing the above title. The work is incomplete, the beginning having been lost with the two pages which contained on their *recto* Iliad II. 1–100. It is a short treatise on Greek grammar, giving an outline of the various parts of speech. The sections which still remain deal with the personal and possessive pronouns (ἀντωνυμίαι), prepositions (προθέσεις), adverbs (ἐπιρρήματα), and conjunctions (σύνδεσμοι). The pronouns are declined in full and some examples are given of their use; the prepositions are enumerated, with the cases which they govern; the adverbs and conjunctions are classified according to their meanings, and specimens are given of each variety. It cannot be said that this treatise adds anything tangible to our knowledge of Greek grammar. It is too much a mere skeleton outline, and, as the only examples quoted in it are taken from Homer, it does not, as so many grammarians do, contribute even a fragment to the remains of classical literature.

The work bears, in the title affixed to it, the name of Tryphon. This grammarian flourished, according to Suidas, in the latter half of the 1st century B.C. Suidas gives a long list of the works written by him, and others, not included in that list, are quoted by various writers, especially Apollonius. All the extant fragments are collected and discussed by A. von Velsen (*Tryphonis grammatici Alexandrini fragmenta*, Berlin, 1853). Among the works thus quoted are treatises περὶ προθέσεων, περὶ ἐπιρρημάτων, and περὶ συνδέσμων, and von Velsen shows good reason to believe that there was also a treatise περὶ ἀντωνυμιῶν from which several citations are made. We thus have remains of works by Tryphon on each of the four subjects included in the present document. It is certain, however, that these works were not identical with that contained in the MS. now before us. The extant fragments show clearly that the original works of Tryphon treated the subject-matter at much greater length, discussing doubtful points, suggesting derivations, and propounding difficulties; whereas the present document contains nothing but the barest outlines of grammar. There is no proof that Tryphon himself ever composed such a handbook of grammar; but it does not follow that the ascription of this little treatise to him is wholly false. Two explanations are possible. In the first place, the fact that the extant fragments contain no mention of such a work only goes a very little way towards proving that he never wrote one. Later grammarians would have no occasion to refer to a skeleton outline, containing little or no disputable matter, when they had the fuller treatises of the same author at their disposal. The second, and perhaps more probable, hypothesis is that this document is an abstract made by a student for his own private purposes from the longer works or work of Tryphon. There would be nothing more unreasonable in appending Tryphon's name to such an abstract than there is in a schoolboy of the present day heading his note-book on Greek or Latin grammar with the name of "Roby's Latin Grammar" or "Goodwin's Greek Syntax" when he has been making an analysis of either of these works. In this case one has only to suppose that the compiler of the abstract collected the plain facts of grammar from Tryphon's work, and omitted the discussions and disquisitions upon doubtful points. It may perhaps be finally suggested that, although Tryphon's remarks on prepositions, adverbs, conjunctions, &c., are referred to by separate titles, it does not necessarily follow that they were independent works; and as we find these four sections here combined into one outline of grammar, so it is not improbable that the original from which they were abstracted was a work on grammar at large, of which the treatises on these subjects were sections.

The manuscript is written, as already stated, in three pages or columns. The hand is not the same as that of the Homer, but is semi-cursive, of moderate size, and probably not much later in date, in the 5th or perhaps the 6th century. The writing in itself is plain, but the papyrus is in some places very deeply stained, which makes decipherment difficult and occasionally impossible. Each section of the work has its title, which does not, however, stand in a line by itself, but in the same line with the last words of the preceding section. Grammatical forms quoted in the course of it are usually marked by a line drawn above them, though there are occasional errors in the use of this sign. No accents or breathings are used; but there is a certain amount of punctuation by means of dots, which are placed in the line of writing, and the words are generally separated from one another. The orthography is generally correct, but there are a few natural blunders.

The autotype plate represents the lower half of the first column of the treatise.

Col. 1. ὧδε του . . . . πρώτου
προσώπου νὼ [καὶ] νῶι, γενικῆς καὶ δοτικῆς σφῶ[ν]
καὶ σφῶϊν· δευτέρου προσώπου, ὀρθῆς καὶ αἰτιατικῆς σφὼ
καὶ σφῶϊ· τρίτου προσώπου, ὀρθῆς καὶ αἰτιατικῆς οὐκ ἔνεισ[ι].
5 δοτικῆς δὲ σφωίν, αἰτιατικῆς δὲ σφωέ. ἀμφότεραι κα-
τ' ἔγκλισιν ἐκφέρονται. πληθυντικαί. ὀρθῆς πτώσεως ἡμεῖς
ὑμεῖς σφεῖς, γενικῆς ἡμῶν ὑμῶν σφῶν ἢ σφέ[ων],
δοτικῆς ἡμῖν ὑμῖν σφὶν ἢ σφ[ίσι]ν, αἰτιατικῆς ἡμᾶ[ς]
ὑμᾶς σφᾶς ἢ σφέας, κλητικ[ῆ]s δευτέρου προσώπου
10 ὑμεῖς. τούτων δὲ τῶν ἀντων[υμ]ιῶν εἰσί τινες αἱ τοῦ
πρώτου προσώπου δεικτικῶς λ[εγόμε]ναι, αἱ δὲ ἀναφορικῶς·
δεικτικῶς μὲν αἱ ἐπὶ παρόντων προσώπων λεγόμεναι,
οἷον, οὗτός τοι Διόμηδες ἀπὸ στρατοῦ ἔρχεται ἀνήρ· ἢ ἐπὶ προειρημένων πραγμάτων ἢ μελλόντων ῥηθήσεσθαι, οἷον,
15 ἀλλὰ τόδ' αἰνὸν ἄχος κραδίην καὶ θυμὸν ἱκάνει ὁππότ' ἂν

2. σφῶν καὶ σφῶιν: the scribe has inadvertently given the genitive and dative of the dual of the second person, instead of those of the first, and he has omitted them in their proper place. The text should run νῶν καὶ νῶϊν· δευτέρου προσώπου, ὀρθῆς καὶ αἰτιατικῆς, σφὼ καὶ σφῶϊ, γενικῆς καὶ δοτικῆς σφῶν καὶ σφῶϊν· τρίτου κ.τ.λ.

3. καὶ αἰτιατικῆς: MS. καιτιατικης, and so again, apparently, in the next line.

4. αἰτιατικῆς: apparently should be γενικῆς. There is some confusion in the writing and perhaps the word was meant to be corrected.

5. σφωίν . . . σφωέ: at first written σφωε . . . σφωιν in the MS., but corrected.

13. οὗτός τοι κ.τ.λ.: Homer, Il. X. 341, where Aristarchus read τις for τοι, but all existing MSS. have τοι.

15, 16. ἀλλὰ τόδ' κ.τ.λ.: Homer, Il. XV. 208, 9.

ἰσόμορον καὶ ὁμῇ πεπρωμένον αἴσῃ. ἀναφορικῶς δὲ αἱ ἐ-
πὶ προειρημένων προσώπων λεγόμεναι, οὗτοι ἄρ' ἡγεμόνες Δαναῶν καὶ κοίρανοι ἦσαν· ἢ ἐπὶ προειρημένων πρα-
[γμάτω]ν, οἷον, οὐ γὰρ ἐγώ γέ τί φημι τέλος χαριέστερον εἶ-
20 [να]ι, ἢ ὅταν εὐφροσύν[η μὲν ἔ]χῃ κάτα δῆμον ἅπαντα,
καὶ μετ' ὀλίγον, τοῦτό τί [μοι κάλλιστ]ον ἐνὶ φρεσὶν εἴδεται εἶ[ναι].
παρὰ δὲ τῷ ποιητῇ ἀντὶ τῶ[ν π]ροϋποκειμένων πραγμ[ά]-
των τοῦ τρίτου προσ[ώπου ἀντ]ωνυμιῶν τίθενται λέξε[ις]
μονοσύλλαβοι ὅμοιοι [τοῖς ἄρ]θροις ἴσα .. αμουσαι αὖται, [ἀρσ]-
25 ενικαῖς μὲν ὁ θηλυκαῖ[ς δ]ὲ ἡ οὐδετέραις δὲ τό, καὶ τούτων πτώσεις καθ' ἕκαστον ἀριθμὸν διαφέρουσαι. αἱ δὲ
αὐταὶ κατὰ διαφορὰν καὶ δεῖξιν λέγονται. ἐπὶ δὲ τῶν ἀντωνυμιῶν αἱ μὲν κατ' ἀντίθεσιν λέγονται αἱ δὲ ἀπολελυμένως·
κατ' ἀντίθεσιν μὲν ὅταν ἕτερον ἀντικέηται πρόσωπον,
30 οἷον, ὑμῖν μὲν θεοὶ δοῖεν Ὀλύμπια δώματ' ἔχοντες ἐκ-
πέρσαι Πριάμοιο πόλιν εὖ δ' οἴκαδ' ἱκέσθαι, παῖδα δ' ἐμοὶ
λύσαιτε φίλην· ἀπολελυμένως δὲ ὅταν ἕτερον μὴ ἀντικέηται πρόσωπον, οἷον, οὐχ ἡμῖν συνθεύσεται ἥδε γε βουλή,
καί, δός μοι ἔτι πρόφρων. ἔχουσι δὲ ἑτέραν δύναμιν αἵ τε
35 αὐτὸς καὶ αὐτὴ καὶ αὐτό, καὶ τούτων πτώσεις καθ' ἕκαστον
ἀριθμὸν διαφέρουσαι. οὐ γὰρ μόνον ἐπὶ τοῦ τρίτου προσώπου
συντάσσονται ἀλλὰ καὶ τοῖς τρισὶ προσώποις τοῖς ἀπαρεμφά-
τοις τὰ γένη ἀφαρμόζουσι συζευγνύμεναι, οἷον, ἐγὼ
αὐτός, σὺ αὐτός, ἲ αὐτός. τῶν δὲ συνάρθρων ἀντωνυμιῶν
40 περὶ δύο θεωρουμένων, περί τε τὸ λέγον πρόσωπον καὶ τὸ
ἔξωθεν προσυπακουόμενον, ὅ εἰσὶν ἀριθμῶν διαφο-
ραί· κατ' ἀμφότερα ἑνικαί, ἐμὸς σὸς ὃς ἤτοι ἐμὸς

16. ἰσόμορον: originally written εισομορον, but the ε appears to be struck out.
17, 18. οὗτοι ἄρ' ἡγεμόνες: Homer, Il. II. 760.
19-21. οὐ γὰρ ἐγώ γέ κ.τ.λ.: Homer, Od. IX. 5, 6, 11.
23. τίθενται: the first two letters are added above the line.
25. οὐδετέραις: corrected in the MS. from ουδετεραις.

26. διαφέρουσαι: MS. apparently διαφορουσαι.
27. δεῖξιν: MS. διξιν.
30-32. ὑμῖν μὲν κ.τ.λ.: Homer, Il. I. 18-20.
33. οὐχ ἡμῖν κ.τ.λ.: Homer, Od. XX. 245.
34. δός μοι ἔτι πρόφρων: Homer, Od. IX. 355.
38. σιζευγνύμεναι: MS. συνζευγνυμενοι.
42. ἀμφότερα: MS. αμφοτεραι.
ἤτοι: written ἤ in the MS., and so in ll. 43, 44.

ΤΕΧΝΗ ΓΡΑΜΜΑΤΙΚΗ.

τεὸς ἑός, ἐμὴ σὴ ἣ ἤτοι ἐμὴ τεὴ
ἑή, ἐμὸν σὸν ὃν ἤτοι ἐμὸν τεὸν ἑόν· ἐντὸς ἑνικαὶ
45 ἐκτὸς δυικαί, κοιναὶ ἀρσενικοῦ καὶ οὐθετέρου ἐμὼ σ[ὼ]
ὤ, καὶ θηλυκῶς ἐμὰ σὰ ἅ, γενικῆς καὶ δοτικῆς
ἐμοῖν σοῖν οἷν, ἐμαῖν σαῖν αἷν· ἐντὸς ἑνικαὶ
[ἐ]κτὸς πληθυντικαί, ἐμοὶ σοὶ οἵ,

Col. 2. ἐμαὶ σαὶ αἵ, ἐμὰ σὰ ἅ· ἐντὸς δυικαὶ ἐκτὸς ἑνικαί, νωΐτε-
50 ρος σφωίτερος, καὶ θηλυκῶς νωιτέρα σφωιτέρα,
καὶ οὐθετέρως νωίτερον σφωίτερον· κατ' ἀμφότερα
δυικαί, ἀρσενικῶς καὶ οὐθετέρως, νωιτέρω σφωιτέρω,
καὶ θηλυκῶς νωιτέρα σφωιτέρα, γενικῆς καὶ δοτικῆς
νωιτέροιν σφωιτέροιν, καὶ θηλυκῶς νωιτέραιν σφωι-
55 τέραιν· ἐντὸς δυικαὶ ἐκτὸς πληθυντικαί, νωίτεροι σφω-
ίτεροι, νωίτεραι σφωίτεραι, νωίτερα σφωίτερα· ἐντὸς
πληθυντικαὶ ἐκτὸς ἑνικαί, ἡμέτερος ὑμέτερος σφέτε-
ρος, καὶ θηλυκῶς ἡμετέρα ὑμετέρα σφετέρα, καὶ
οὐδετέρως ἡμέτερον ὑμέτερον σφέτερον· ἐντὸς
60 πληθυντικαὶ ἐκτὸς δυικαί, κοινὰ ἀρσενικῶν καὶ οὐ-
θετέρων, ἡμετέρω ὑμετέρω σφετέρω, ἡμετέρα
ὑμετέρα σφετέρα, γενικῆς καὶ δοτικῆς ἡμετέροιν
ὑμετέροιν σφετέροιν, ἡμετέραιν ὑμετέραιν σφετέραιν·
κατ' ἀμφότερα πληθυντικαί, ἡμέτεροι ὑμέτεροι σφέ-
65 τεροι, ἡμέτεραι ὑμέτεραι σφέτεραι, ἡμέτερα ὑμέ-
τερα σφέτερα. Πρόθεσις.
πρόθεσίς τί ἐστιν μέρος λόγου ᾧ συμβέβηκε καθ' ἕνα ἀνασχ[η]-

---

43. At the end of the line the words ἢ ἐμὸν σὸν ὃν have been written, but they are struck out, being out of place here.

44, 45. ἐντός relates to the meaning of the pronoun itself, ἐκτός to the shape it takes when used in agreement with some noun. Thus ἐμώ is singular ἐντός, as it refers to an individual person; but it is dual ἐκτός, as being used in agreement with a noun in the dual. Or, as it may be put in another way, the root is singular, the inflexion dual.

45. οὐθετέρου: MS. ουθετερω.

58. σφετέρα: MS. σφωιτερα, which is evidently a slip of the pen, due to the forms in σφωι- which have preceded.

67. συμβέβηκε καθ' ἕνα ἀνασχηματισμόν: MS. συμβεβηκαθ κ.τ.λ., but corrected. It may be questioned whether ανα is not merely a corrupt repetition of ενα, as no such word as ἀνασχηματισμός is given in the lexicons, and καθ' ἕνα σχηματισμόν is the phrase employed in the definition of prepositions in other grammarians (e.g. the scholium to Dionysius in Bekker's Anecdota Graeca, p. 924).

ΤΡΥΦΩΝΟΣ

ματισμὸν ἐκφέρεσθαι καὶ πάντων τῶν τοῦ λόγου μερῶν συνθέσει προτίθεσθαι, ἐν δὲ συντάξει τῶν πλείστων, ὀρθ[ῇ]
70 καὶ κλητικῇ πτώσει οὐ δυνάμενον συντάσσεσθαι οὐδὲ ἐν λογῷ γενναίῳ προτίθεσθαι. προθέσεις δέ εἰσιν $\overline{ιη}$ $\overline{ἀνά}$ $\overline{ἀμφί}$ $\overline{ἀπό}$ $\overline{ἀντί}$ $\overline{διά}$ $\overline{ἐν}$ $\overline{ἐξ}$ $\overline{εἰς}$ $\overline{ἐπί}$ $\overline{κα[τά]}$ $\overline{πρός}$ $\overline{πρό}$ $\overline{περί}$ $\overline{παρά}$ $\overline{μετά}$ $\overline{ὑπέρ}$ $\overline{ὑπό}$ $\overline{σύν}$. τῶν [δὲ] προθέσεων ἀναστροφὴν ἐπιδέχονται $\overline{ἀνά}$ $\overline{ἀπό}$
75 $\overline{ἐπί}$ $\overline{κατά}$ $\overline{περί}$ $\overline{παρά}$ $\overline{μετά}$ $\overline{ὑπέρ}$ $\overline{ὑπό}$. πτώσεσι δὲ ταῖς πλαγίοις συντάσσονται ἐξ αἵδε, $\overline{ἀμφί}$ $\overline{ἐπί}$ $\overline{πρός}$ $\overline{περί}$ $\overline{παρά}$ $\overline{ὑπό}$· γενικῇ καὶ δοτικῇ $\overline{γ}$ αἵδε, $\overline{κατά}$ $\overline{μετά}$ $\overline{ὑπέρ}$· γενικῇ $\overline{ε}$, $\overline{ἀπό}$ $\overline{ἀμφί}$ $\overline{διά}$ $\overline{ἐξ}$ $\overline{πρό}$ καὶ . . . . τικοι $\overline{β}$, $\overline{ἐν}$ $\overline{εἰς}$· δοτικῇ δύο, $\overline{ἐν}$ $\overline{σύν}$· καὶ αἰτιατικῇ $\overline{β}$, $\overline{ἀνά}$
80 $\overline{εἰς}$. Ἐπίρρημα. ἐπίρρημά τίς ἐστιν λέξις καθ' ἕνα σχηματισμὸν ἐκφερομένη, προτακτικὴ καὶ ὑποτακτικὴ ῥήματος ἀσυνθέτου ἐν εἴδεσι θεωρουμένη. τῶν δὲ ἐπιρρημάτων ἃ μέν ἐστιν μεσότητος καὶ ποιότητος δηλωτικά, οἷον καλῶς, σοφῶς, ἄρδην, ἀνέδην, βοτρυδόν, α . . . ια . .
85 νύξ, γνύξ, λάξ, ὀδάξ, ἄν, νῶν, ἀκονιτί, σάφα, μάλα, λικριφίς, ἀμοιβηδίς, ἑλληνιστί, συριστί, ... ἃ δὲ ποσότητος, οἷον δίς, τρίς, πεντάκις, καὶ ἔτι πλεί[ω]· ἃ δὲ χρόνου, ἤδη, νῦν, αὖτις, πάλιν, ἐχθές, τηνίκα, καὶ τὰ ὅμοια· ἃ δὲ εὐχῆς, οἷον αἴθε, εἴθε, βαβαιάξ· τινὰ
90 δὲ ἀπαγορεύσεως, μή, μηκέτι· τινὰ δὲ συγκαταθέσεως, ναί, ναίχι· τοῦ δ' αὐτοῦ εἴδους κατωμοτικά, οἷον νή,

---

70. συντάσπεσθαι: MS. συντασεσθαι.
71. προθέσεις: MS. προθεσις.
72. ἐν: MS. ενα.
    ἐπί: MS. επει, and so again in line 75.
79. σύν: MS. ουν.
    καὶ αἰτιατικῇ: MS. καιτιατικη.
80. τίς: MS. τι.
82. ἐπιρρημάτων: MS. επιρηματων· and so again in l. 100, επιρηματα.
83. ποιότητος: MS. ποιοδητος.
85. νύξ: presumably a scribe's error for πύξ.
    ἄν, νῶν: there is no question as to the reading of the MS., but there must be some blunder, as neither of these words is an adverb.
    μάλα: the reading is very doubtful. The part of the papyrus on which the ends of the lines are written is extremely discoloured, especially in the lower half of the column.
86. ἀμοιβηδίς: MS. αμοιβηδης, which may be intended for either ἀμοιβηδίς or ἀμοιβηδήν.
88. τηνίκα: the first three letters are doubtful.
90. συγκαταθέσεως: MS. συνκαταθεσεως.

ΤΕΧΝΗ ΓΡΑΜΜΑΤΙΚΗ.

.. το μά· κοινὰ λιτῆς ἀπώμοσα..........
... ὡς· ἃ δὲ ἐρωτήσεως.............

Col. 3. ταῦτα καὶ τοπικά ἐστιν παρακελεύσεως, δεῦτε·
95 τὸ δ' αὐτὸ καὶ ῥῆμα γίνεται προστακτικόν· ὁμοιώσεως
ἢ παραβολῆς, ὣς· τὸ δ' αὐτὸ καὶ πλείστας ἔχει δυ-
νάμεις· ἃ δὲ ἐπικελευστικά, ἅπερ οἱ μὲν ἐπι-
φθέγματα καλοῦσιν, οἱ δὲ συνεμφάσεις, οἱ δὲ
σχετλιασμούς, φεῦ, παπαῖ, ὤμοι. φασὶ δὲ κα[ὶ]
100 εἰκασμοῦ τινὰ εἶναι ἐπιρρήματα, ὡς τὸ τυχόν, σχεδόν, ἴσως, τάχα· ἃ δὲ τάξεως, ἑξῆς, χωρίς.
ἐπίρρημα δὲ εἴρηται διὰ τὸ καθ' ἑαυτὸ μὲν λεγόμενον
μὴ ἀποτελεῖν διάνοιαν ἐγγράμματον, προστασ-
σομέν(ου) δὲ ῥήματος ζευγνύμενον ῥῆμα-
105 τι κατὰ τὸ πλεῖστον. Σύνδεσμος.
σύνδεσμός τίς ἐστιν λέξις συνδετικὴ τῶν τοῦ λόγου
μερῶν. τούτων δ' εἴδη πλείονα. οἱ μὲν γὰρ αὐτῶν
εἰσὶν συμπλεκτικοί, οἱ δὲ διαζευκτικοί, οἱ δὲ συν-
απτικοί, οἱ δὲ παρασυναπτικοί, ἄλλοι δὲ συλλογιστικοί,
110 οἱ δὲ ἀπορηματικοί, καὶ τελευταῖοι παραπληρωματικ[οί].
συμπλεκτικοὶ μὲν οὖν εἰσιν οἵδε, μέν, δέ, τε, καί, ἀ[λλά],
ἢ μέν, ἢ δέ, ἰδέ, αὐτάρ, ἀτάρ, ἤτοι, κεν, ἄν· διαζευ[κτικοὶ]
δέ, ἤ, ἤτοι, ἠέ· αἰτιολογικοὶ δέ, οὕνεκα, τούν[εκα],
ἐπεάν, ἵνα, χάριν, ὄφρα, ὅπως, ὅτι, γάρ, διότι, καθ[ότι],
115 καθόσον· συναπτικοὶ δέ, εἰ, εἴπερ, εἰ δέ, εἰ δέ περ, ε[ἰ δή].
παρασυναπτικοὶ δέ, ἐπεί, ἐπείπερ, ἐπειδή, ἐπειδ[άν],

92. The readings in this line are rather doubtful.

96. παραβολῆς: corrected in the MS. from παραβολως.

πλείστας ἔχει δυνάμεις: we know from an anonymous grammarian quoted by Hermann, *De emend. gramm.* p. 463 (von Velsen, p. 45) that Tryphon enumerated thirty different uses of ὡς.

101. Between σχεδόν and ἴσως a character is written in the MS., apparently either ο or α, but it must be due to a scribe's blunder.

104. Before ζευγνύμενον there is a blank space capable of holding three or four letters, but there are no traces of writing in it.

106. τις: MS. τι. συνδετική: MS. συνδεκτικη.

109. συλλογιστικοί: corrected in the MS. from συνλογιστικοι.

113. αἰτιολογικοί: in the MS. the letters following the λ are erased, except the termination -οι, and over the erasure are written the letters ιγ, so that the word reads αιτιολιγοι; but the correction must be due to a misapprehension.

ἐπειπερδή· συλλογιστικοὶ δὲ ἄρα, ἀλλὰ μήν, τ[οιγάρ],
τοιγαροῦν, τοιγάρτοι· ἀπορηματικοὶ δέ, ἄρα, κᾶτα . . . . .
εἶτα, ἠέ· παραπληρωματικοὶ δέ, ἦ, δή, ἄρα, νύν, ...
120 θήν, οὖν, μήν, τοί γε, πέρ, τάρ. εἰσὶ δέ τινες ὑ[πο]-
θετικοὶ σύνδεσμοι, αἰ κέν, εἰ κέν, ἐάν, εἰ δ' ἄν.

Τρύφωνος τέχνη γραμματική.

117. συλλογιστικοί : MS. συνλογιστικοι.

118. κᾶτα : we know from Apollonius *De Conjunctionibus*, p. 496, 18 *seq.* that Tryphon, in his treatise περὶ συνδέσμων, denied that καὶ εἶτα could be contracted into κᾶτα, holding that they must become κεῖτα, on the analogy of κεῖχον and other such words ; and accordingly he maintained that κᾶτα was formed from καί as δῆτα from δή, or else was a primary word. *Cf.* von Velsen, pp. 37-39. Hence, supposing the present work to be an abstract of Tryphon, it is probable that this is the word on which, in the original work, the discussion occurred. The end of this line, as well as that of the following one, is lost through the mutilation of the papyrus.

122. γραμματική : MS. γραμματικοι, which may be a blunder for either γραμματική or γραμματικοῦ, but more probably the former.

HERODAS.

ADDENDUM.

THE following is the text of the detached fragments of the MS. of Herodas, mentioned on p. 6 of this volume. None contains a complete line, but two are of some size and interest. No. 6 contains a passage, apparently of an autobiographical description, in which is introduced the name of Hipponax, together with the term Ξουθίδαι (=Ἴωνες, cf. Hesych. s. v.); but unfortunately the context is mutilated. The same fragment contains the title of another poem, Ἀπονηστιζόμεναι. The rest of the fragments are less valuable, but they include a new proverb, Λάτμιον κνώσσειν (1 l. 7), and the rare words ἄναυλος (1 l. 4, apparently a ἅπαξ λεγόμενον derivative from αὐλή), ἀρνευτήρ (2 l. 3) and γλήχων (7 l. 5).

(1) FRAGMENT (fitted together from several pieces) containing the greater part of a column, complete in height (4¾ in.) and 3¾ in. in greatest width. Perhaps a part of the eighth poem, and possibly the immediate sequel of the three lines which end col. 41, in which case [αυστηθ]ι should be read in l. 3.

```
     . . . . . υσον εσδυς κως δ ατρυτε κου καμνις
     . . . . . ευρα κνωσσους αι δε νυκτες εννεωροι
     . . . . . ι φημι και αψον ει θελις λυχνον
     . . . . . ην αναυλον χοιρον ες νομην πεμψ . .
5    . . . . . θρυζε και κνω μεχρις ευ παραστα . . .
     . . . . . . μα τωι σκιπωνι μαλθακον θωμα[ι]
     . . . . . . εγαλλί κα[ι] συ Λατμιον κνωσσις
```

3. αψον: MS. at first αστησον, but the 2nd, 4th, and 5th letters are dotted, and the τ is altered to a ψ.
5. The second letter is doubtful.

......α σε τρυχ[ου]σιν αλλα μην στεμμ[α]
......ιζομε[σθ]α βα.ις ουχ ημιν
10 ......ηι ετιμα..μοσιριων διλη
......ουτεμοσ....ει θελις αννᾶ
......ου.........φρενας βοσκις
          ηθ
......τιν.........αραι τοσωι ομ...
......σο.........ντεκευκερως
15 ....ην..της βησσης
............μεν κ[αι] γαρ εσσωμαι
............ισαι χ[ειρ]ες αιπολοι πλε...
............νηπα..ριων τε ποιευ...

9. βα.ις: the α is doubtful.
10. The μ after the lacuna is doubtful.
13. At the end of the line the letters ηθ are written above the line, apparently as correction of ομ. The letter following ομ appears to be ι or ν.

15-18. The earlier letters of these lines are on a detached fragment of papyrus, which appears from its texture to belong to this place.

(2) FRAGMENT from the top of a column, with beginnings of lines; measures 2½ in. by 1¾ in., a large part being margin.

   ωσπερ τελευμεν εγ.......
   χοι μεν μετωποις.......
   εκοπτον αρνευτηρ.......
   οι δ υπτι ερριπτευντ......
5 εισεν γελως τε καν ιη....
   καγω δοκεον δισμ.....
   .....ναλεσθαι κη.....
   ....στη.....

5. εισεν: the σ is added above the line.

(3) FRAGMENT containing middles of lines; measures 3½ in. by 1¼ in. (for the greater part only ¾ in.).

   ....ηγω ουκ εσυλευν....
   ....ν αλλης δρυος....
   ....δαμ..ι καρτα....
   ....να..ποιουν....

ADDENDUM. 119

```
       5 . . . . . . . . σιον με . . . .
         . . . . . . . . αιμαλ . . . .
         . . . . . . . . κροκωτ . . .
         . . . . . . . . επτησα . . . .
         . . . . . . . σδενεβ . . . .
      10 . . . . . . . . νκυπα . . . .
         . . . . . . . . αμφικν . . . .
         . . . . . . [κο]θορνου[ς] . . .
         . . . . . . . . μεν το . . . .
         . . . . . . . ωρηνιμ . . . .
      15 . . . . . . . . ολωπο . . . .
         . . . . . . . . σσεωσο . . . .
```

6. The αι may also be read as ν.
7. The first κ is doubtful.
11. The ν is doubtful.

15. The first o is so corrected in the MS. from ω.
16. The o is corrected in the MS. from ω.

(4) FRAGMENT containing beginnings of lines; 1¼ in. by 1 in.

```
         . . . . . . .
         αν . . . . .
         ιαμ . . . .
         ισσι . . . .
       5 . κα . . . .
         σα . . . . .
         θι . . . . .
```

(5) TWO small contiguous fragments, from the middle of a column, measuring together 1½ in. by 1¼ in.

```
         . . . . μαι δε τ[η]ν νεην . . . .
         . . . . μφωτ . νδορεα . . . . .
         . . . . ονελη . . το ενδυ . . . .
         . . . . ωδε των αρωδι . . . . .
       5 . . . . ναι τα της φ . . . . .
         . . . . λου δω . . . . . . .
         . . . . πολοι μ . . . . . .
         . . . . . ελευ . . . . . . .
```

120   *HERODAS.*

(6) FRAGMENT from the top of a column; 3 in. by 2½ in.

  .... κλεος ναι μουσαν η μ επεα κ.....
  . εγ εξ ιαμβων η με δευτερη γν....
  [η]μας μεθ Ιππωνακτα τον παλα[ι].....
  [τ]α κυλλ ' αιδιν Ξουθιδαις επιουσι[ν]
5   Απονηστιζομεναι
  [ε]ζεσθε πασαι κου το παιδιον δοξ...
  . αι π . οσευετειραν [κ]αι γλυκην......
  .... αιδρη την ετοιμον ο.....
  .... ισμησε .. ισματων ....
10 .... ινα....... νυτο....
  .... η........ πεπο....
  .... εσκο....

3. ημας: the reading is doubtful, except the s. sumably to show the right division of the
4. There seems to be a dot after κυλλ, pre- words.

(7) FRAGMENT from the bottom of a column, with beginnings of lines;
2 in. by ¾ in.

  . ερ......
  ευτη....
  ευτ.....
  τιθεσ....
5 γληχ[ω]....

(8) TWO fragments containing beginnings of lines, one from the top of a column, measuring 2¼ in. by 1¾ in., the other from the bottom, measuring 1¾ in. by 1½ in. The texture of the perpendicular fibres of papyrus on the *verso* shows that they belong to the same column. The interval between them is of doubtful size, but 18 is the normal number of lines in a column.

  τα δεινα.....
  ερρ εκ προ....
  οληι κατι....
  κηγω μ.....
5 θανευμ.....

4. κηγω: corrected from κωγω.

ADDENDUM.

       μαρτυρ . . . . .
       ο δ ιπεν . . . .
       και του τι . . . .
       . . ναδ . . . . .
10   . . . .

       . . . .
       . . νοσα . . . . .
       τα μελεα . . . .
15   τιλευσιν ε . . . .
       το μη να . . . .
       πολλων τ . . . .
       κη τωι γ . . . .

(9) FRAGMENT measuring 3¼ in. by 1 in.; the margin stretches 1½ in. above the first line of which any letter is preserved. Apparently beginnings of lines, but there is some irregularity of writing and surface which suggest that possibly some letters have been obliterated along the whole length of the papyrus, to the left of those which are preserved.

       βρεγ . . . . .
       λημ . . . . .
       τα εργ . . . .
       πιρα δ . . . .
5   τηι οικι . . . .
       στηθι . . . .
       λουσον . . . .
       αγον . . . . .
       ακρη . . . . .
10   . ιδεδ . . . . .
       . . σφα . . . .

(10) FRAGMENT from the top of a column; 1¼ in. by ½ in. The texture and appearance of the papyrus suggest that it belongs to the same part of the MS. as fragments 2 and 3, but its exact place cannot be identified.

       . . . . ωσεχ . . . .
       . . . . αδη . . . .
       . . . . εζον . . . .

(11) FRAGMENT containing ends of lines; 2 in. by ½ in. After l. 5 there is a blank space which may indicate the beginning of a new poem; but it may also be accounted for by the next line being a short one. There is a short space of blank papyrus also below the last line, which may be due either to this being the bottom of a column or to a couple of short lines.

$$\ldots\ldots \lambda\kappa o\nu$$
$$\ldots\ldots \upsilon$$
$$\ldots\ldots \epsilon\upsilon\nu\tau o$$
$$\ldots\ldots \nu\upsilon\nu\tau o$$
$$5 \ldots\ldots o\chi\theta o\upsilon\varsigma$$

$$\ldots\ldots \nu o\varsigma$$
$$\ldots\ldots\ldots \eta\sigma a\nu$$
$$\ldots\ldots\ldots \tau\iota$$

www.ingramcontent.com/pod-product-compliance
Lightning Source LLC
Chambersburg PA
CBHW022126160426
43197CB00009B/1168